LIN

WESTERN ISL

D0334319

Readers are requested to take great care of the books while in their
possession, and to point out any defects they may notice in them
to the Librarian.
This book is issued for   days and should be
returned on or before   but an extension
of the period

SUTTON POCKET HISTORIES

THE FALKLANDS WAR

MICHAEL PARSONS

SUTTON PUBLISHING

First published in 2000 by
Sutton Publishing Limited · Phoenix Mill
Thrupp · Stroud · Gloucestershire · GL5 2BU

British Library Cataloguing in Publication Data
A catalogue record for this book is available from the British
Library.

ISBN 0-7509-2354-7

Cover picture: 45 Commando Royal Marines march into Stanley.
(The Defence Picture Library.)

Typeset in 11/14 pt New Baskerville.
Typesetting and origination by
Sutton Publishing Limited.
Printed in Great Britain by
Cox & Wyman, Reading, Berkshire.

Contents

List of Dates

1501   Amerigo Vespucci sights islands that may have been the Falklands (Malvinas).

1520   Esteban Gomez, the captain of one of Magellan's ships, sights islands that may have been the Falklands.

1540   One of the ships from a Spanish expedition under Francisco de Camargo winters in islands that may have been the Falklands.

1592   The Englishman John Davis sights islands that may have been the Falklands.

1600   Sebald van Weerdt, a Dutchman, sights islands that may well have been the Jason group of islands to the north-west of the Falklands.

1690   Captain John Strong enters the sound between the islands and names it Falkland Sound, and lands on the islands.

1764   Louis Antoine de Bougainville sets up a French colony at Port Louis on East Falkland.

1765   John Byron lands on Saunders Island, which lies off West Falkland, and claims sovereignty over the group for Britain.

1766   A British settlement is established at Port Egmont on Saunders Island.

1767   Bougainville agrees to abandon the colony, in return for compensation from Spain. Port Louis becomes Puerto Soledad.

1770   A Spanish force expels the British from Port Egmont.

1771   Spain returns Port Egmont to the British.

1774	The British depart from Port Egmont for reasons of economy, but leave a lead plaque claiming sovereignty.
1775	Captain Cook discovers South Georgia.
1811	The Spanish evacuate the Falklands.
1816	Argentina claims independence as the United Provinces of the Rio de la Plata.
1820	David Jewett (aka Daniel Jewitt) takes possession of the islands for the United Provinces.
1823/6	Louis Vernet establishes a settlement.
1829	Vernet appointed governor of the Malvinas.
1831	Vernet seizes three American ships that were hunting seals in areas over which he claimed authority. In December the USS *Lexington* attacks Puerto Soledad and proclaims the islands free of all government.
1832	New governor Mestivier appointed, and then murdered. Captain Pinedo sent to re-establish authority.
1833	Captain James Onslow annexes the islands for Britain. Buenos Aires protests.
1843	Letter patent proclaiming the islands British.
1852	Falkland Islands Company given royal charter.
1908	Letter patent establishes sovereignty over South Georgia, South Sandwich Islands and British Antarctic territory.
1960	UN Resolution calling for decolonisation.
1965	UN Resolution 2065 asserts that the Falklands/Malvinas constitute a colony and calls on Britain and Argentina to negotiate taking account of the islanders' interests.
1966	Private Argentine 'occupation' attempt at Stanley airfield.
1968	Memorandum of Understanding is agreed official level. Lord Chalfont visits the islands. Parliament undertakes to make no change against the islanders' wishes.
1971	Communications Agreement.
1974	Fuel provided by Argentina.

1975   Shackleton survey commissioned.

1976   Argentine base secretly set up on Southern Thule.

1977   British secretly send a submarine and two frigates to South Atlantic.

1981   Ridley visit to establish support for leaseback. Later Parliament re-affirms 'paramountcy' of islanders' wishes. In December, Argentine junta under Galtieri, Anaya and Lami Dozo seizes power. First visit of Argentine businessman Constantino Davidoff to South Georgia.

1982   **February.** New York talks establish permanent negotiation commission.

       March. Davidoff workers land on South Georgia illegally. HMS *Endurance* sent to South Georgia. Argentine naval vessels sent to 'protect' the workers.

       2 April. Argentine forces occupy the Falkland Islands.

       3 April. Debate in the House of Commons. UN Resolution 502. Argentine forces take South Georgia.

       5 April. Lord Carrington, Humphrey Atkins and Richard Luce resign. Ships of the Royal Navy, including the aircraft carriers HMS *Hermes* and HMS *Invincible*, leave Portsmouth and elsewhere.

       8 April. Haig arrives in London to begin diplomatic 'shuttle'.

       9 April. Haig arrives in Buenos Aires.

       10 April. EEC declares sanctions against Argentina.

       12 April. Britain declares maritime exclusion zone 200 miles around Falklands.

       19 April. EEC foreign ministers declare support for Britain.

       23 April. Britain warns Argentina that any warship or military aircraft representing a threat to the task force would be dealt with accordingly.

25 April. South Georgia recaptured, *Santa Fe* damaged.

29 April. Argentina rejects Haig proposals.

30 April. Britain declares total exclusion zone.
US announces support for Britain.

1 May. First British attacks.

2 May. Argentine cruiser *General Belgrano* sunk.

4 May. HMS *Sheffield* hit by Exocet missile.

7 May. British government warns Argentina that any warships or military aircraft more than 12 miles from Argentine coast could be regarded as hostile. UN Secretary-General begins talks with Britain and Argentina.

14/15 May. Raid on Pebble Island supported by naval gunfire. Several Argentine Pucara aircraft damaged or destroyed.

16 May. Final British proposals worked out.

17 May. Proposals sent to Argentina.

18 May. Argentine government rejects British proposals.

20 May. UN Secretary-General admits failure of UN talks.

21 May. Beachhead established at San Carlos.
HMS *Ardent* sunk, fifteen Argentine planes shot down.

23 May. HMS *Antelope* damaged (explodes and sinks next day). Seven more Argentine aircraft destroyed.

25 May. HMS *Coventry* sunk by air attack and container ship *Atlantic Conveyor* destroyed by Exocet missile.

27 May. British forces move forwards to Teal Inlet and Mount Kent.

28 May. British victory at Battle of Goose Green (2 Para).

1 June. 5 Infantry Brigade arrive at San Carlos.

4 June. Britain and USA veto UN call for immediate cease-fire.

8 June. Royal Fleet Auxiliaries *Sir Galahad* and *Sir Tristram* bombed at Fitzroy.

11/12 June. Mount Harriet, Two Sisters and Mount Longdon taken by British forces. HMS *Glamorgan* hit by land-launched Exocet.

13/14 June. Tumbledown Mountain, Wireless Ridge and Mount William taken by British forces.

14 June. General Menéndez surrenders to Major-General Jeremy Moore.

17 June. Galtieri resigns.

20 June. Southern Thule retaken. EEC lifts economic sanctions against Argentina.

22 June. General Bignone replaces Galtieri.

25 June. Rex Hunt returns to Port Stanley.

26 July. Ceremony at St Paul's in London.

12 October. Victory parade in London.

4 November. A resolution calling for a peaceful solution to the sovereignty dispute voted by UN General Assembly.

1983   **January.** Franks report published. **October.** Radical Raúl Alfonsín elected President of Argentina.

1984   Talks between Argentina and Britain in Berne fail.

1985   New Falkland Islands Constitution.

1986   Britain announces 150-mile Falkland Islands Interim Conservation and Management Zone. Argentina protests.

1989   Newly elected Argentine President Carlos Menem agrees to talks under 'sovereignty umbrella'.

1990   Full diplomatic relations restored.

1995   Joint agreement on oil exploration and exploitation.

1998   Menem visits London, and Prince Charles visits Buenos Aires and the Falklands.

1999   First Argentine tourists allowed into the Falklands. **October.** First direct flight from Argentina to the Falklands since the war. Thatcher confirms Chilean support in 1982.

Map 1: The South Atlantic. Redrawn from *The Falkland Islands Review*, London, HMSO, 1983, p. 106.

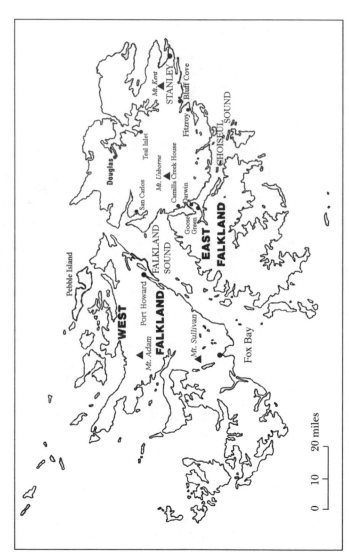

Map 2: The Falkland Islands. Redrawn from *The Falklands Campaign: The Lessons*, London, HMSO, 1982, p. 8.

ONE

Introduction

War is always a failure
Archbishop of Canterbury, January 1983

Outdated neo-colonial adventure, incomprehensible anachronism, courageous stand for international order and peace, fight for freedom and democracy, moment of national greatness . . . There have been a whole range of interpretations of the real meaning of the Falklands War (2 April to 14 June 1982), but there is no doubt that it was an exceptional, perhaps even unique, moment in the history of both Britain and Argentina. It is also referred to among other names as the Falklands conflict, the South Atlantic conflict of 1982, the Falklands crisis or the *guerra de Malvinas*. War was never formally declared (but then most post-Second World War conflicts have not been preceded by formal declarations of war), but it was a war, although a brief affair, in which 255 British servicemen and civilians and over 650 Argentines lost their lives, and many more on both sides were wounded.

1

In some ways the war seemed to belong more to the nineteenth than to the twentieth century. Some of Britain's critics saw it as a kind of last fling of late Victorian neo-colonialism. Britain's actions were compared with the gunboat diplomacy of Lord Palmerston. To begin with, the crisis was not always taken very seriously, and a number of people thought there was a Gilbert and Sullivan flavour to it, although others feared it could turn into Wagnerian tragedy.

Yet for many in Britain the issue was clear-cut. Argentina had 'barged in' (the alliteration of 'Argie' and 'argy-bargy' was irresistible) and taken British territory inhabited by British people, and they had to be removed. There was a strong appeal to powerful traditional values that seemed to have dulled during the 1960s and 1970s. An almost forgotten vocabulary returned in strength – patriotism, principles, duty, courage and resolution – as if the sense of decline that had pervaded the 1970s had vanished, swept away by the predominant mood of determination and confidence. For Argentina, the occupation of the islands put an end to an intolerably long period during which its territorial integrity had been violated. It was almost a mystical experience. President Reagan seemed quite unable to understand why two of the USA's friends were ready to fight over what he rather disparagingly – and somewhat inaccurately – called an 'ice-cold bunch of rocks'. Perhaps the answer was oil, thought those who found it hard to accept that the real issue was something so abstract as national honour and pride or the principle that international law must be upheld and that aggression must not be allowed to pay.

The fighting itself ranged from ultra-modern missile engagements to infantry battles culminating in close combat. It was a war of Exocets and bayonets, of the very latest Sidewinders launched to deadly effect from Harrier 'jump jets', on the one hand, and the 'poor bloody infantryman' having to march to battle with a heavy pack on his back, on the other. Both governments received overwhelming public support. Margaret Thatcher's personal popularity soared upwards, and in Argentina, bitter trade-union protest demonstrations gave way in the space of a couple of days to enthusiastic cheers of joy from huge crowds.

This slim volume represents a daunting challenge: to tell the story of the Falklands War, the events leading up to it and the way it was reported and understood at the time, and to recall what has happened since. It has meant leaving some things out and relating other points very briefly. For readers who want to know more, there is a selective guide to further reading.

TWO

The Sovereignty Dispute

The Falkland Islands lie some 300 miles off the east coast of Argentina, and about 7,500 miles from Britain. The population in 1982 was a little over 1,800. A number of smaller islands to the east and south-east, while legally separate from the Falklands, are administered from the capital of the Falkland Islands at Port Stanley. These dependencies now comprise South Georgia and the South Sandwich Islands. There are no permanent inhabitants.

The question of sovereignty over the Falkland Islands has been a source of tension between Britain and Argentina for over 200 years, although the intensity of the dispute has varied considerably. In 1982 perhaps the most significant feature of the dispute was that most British people were only vaguely aware of it – if indeed they were aware of it at all – whereas to Argentines it was a matter of national pride, liable to generate great emotion. Officially, neither the British nor the Argentines entertained the slightest doubt about the validity of their respective claims.

There is some uncertainty as to who first sighted the islands. The Argentines say that it was Esteban Gomez, who sailed with Magellan in 1520. British sources claim that the first sighting was made by John Davis in 1592. In any case, the question is largely academic in a discussion of British or Argentine rights, since discovery without effective settlement would not be considered sufficient to claim sovereignty.

The first recorded landing on the islands was probably made by Captain John Strong in 1690. It was Captain Strong, too, who named the passage between the two main islands Falkland Sound, in honour of Viscount Falkland, the Treasurer of the Navy. The islands were frequently visited by French sailors from the city of St Malo in Brittany, and the islands were often referred to as the 'Malouines' in recognition of this. The Spanish name for the islands, the 'Malvinas', is derived from the French name.

In 1764 a French settlement called Port Louis was established under Louis Antoine de Bougainville on East Falkland. A short while later, in January 1765, Captain John Byron (the poet's grandfather) landed on Saunders Island, off the north coast of West Falkland, and claimed the islands for Britain. He named the harbour where he had dropped anchor

Port Egmont after the First Lord of the Admiralty. In January the following year Captain John McBride arrived to found a settlement.

In the meantime, the Spanish were alarmed at news of the French settlement, as they claimed that South America was a restricted area where only themselves and the Portuguese had the right to settle. The dispute was resolved peacefully. Port Louis was handed over to Spain in exchange for substantial compensation, and a Spanish governor installed in 1767. Port Louis became Puerto Soledad.

In 1769 a British ship patrolling the sea around the Falkland Islands encountered a Spanish vessel, and the British captain, Hunt, told the Spanish ship to leave. The Spanish Governor of Puerto Soledad in turn ordered the British to leave, and sent two ships from Buenos Aires to enforce the order. Two ships were not enough, and in 1770 five frigates arrived with over 1,000 men and the British were forced to abandon Port Egmont.

The British were incensed by this action and demanded reparation, and for several months Britain, France and Spain were on the brink of war. The Prime Minister, Lord North, seemed prepared to accept some kind of compromise, but his opponents demanded a more robust response. Samuel Johnson was brought in to put the case for peace and refute the strident cries for war made by Lord Chatham and his supporters. Spain was prepared to apologise for the way in which the expulsion had taken place, claiming that the force had been sent by the Governor of Buenos Aires without authority from the Government, but was unwilling to concede sovereignty. Spain had assumed the support of France in all its preparations for war with Britain, but Louis XV informed Charles III of Spain that he did not wish to be drawn into war, so to all intents and purposes Spain was forced to back down, agreeing to restore the *status quo ante*, although declaring that this decision could in no way affect the question of sovereignty.

It has been claimed that a secret agreement was made between Lord North's Government and Spain, to the effect that once the hue and cry had died down the British would quietly abandon the settlement. No documentary evidence has ever been found for this, which is perhaps hardly surprising. It seems that the Spanish diplomat involved in the negotiations did indeed believe Britain intended to vacate the islands, but that in itself proves nothing. Perfidious Albion? Misunderstanding? We will probably never know.

In any case, the Spanish kept their word and the settlement was formally returned to the British in 1771. Only three years later, in 1774, ostensibly as part of what might be referred to today as a 'cost-cutting exercise', the settlement was abandoned, although a notice was erected, formally declaring British sovereignty over the Falkland Islands.

Spain maintained a settlement at Puerto Soledad until the Napoleonic wars, when her authority over her overseas possessions was weakened. On the mainland an autonomous government of the Provinces of the River Plate was set up on 25 May 1810 to administer the viceroyalty, and in 1811 the Spanish garrison and settlement were withdrawn. In 1816 an assembly met and formally declared the country independent as the United Provinces of the Rio de la Plata.

In 1820 Captain David Jewett (also known as Daniel Jewitt) asserted sovereignty over the Falkland Islands in the name of the Buenos Aires Government. The United Provinces claimed that they had inherited sovereignty from Spain. In 1823 a German citizen of French origin, Louis Vernet, was given fishing and other rights. He realised that he could only make a success of the venture if he could effectively control access to the islands and the surrounding seas, and on his request the Government of the United Provinces gave him the authority he needed by appointing him governor in 1829. Britain protested, declaring that the new states of South America had no more right to sovereignty than Spain had had before the collapse of its South American empire.

Meanwhile, Louis Vernet was finding it difficult to enforce exclusive fishing and sealing rights. In 1831 he seized three American ships, which he claimed had been hunting seals illegally, and he took the master of one of the ships to Buenos Aires for trial. The United States Consul in Buenos Aires, however, contested the right of the Buenos Aires Government to sovereignty over the islands. It followed that Vernet had no right to seize a United States' ship and had therefore been guilty of piracy. The Consul accordingly informed the captain of the USS *Lexington*, which happened to be in Buenos Aires, of what had happened, and the warship proceeded to Puerto Soledad, took a few prisoners, destroyed the settlement's guns and declared the islands 'free of all government'.

Buenos Aires appointed Juan Mestivier to take Vernet's place. Once again, Britain protested, and gave orders to Captain Onslow of HMS *Clio* to sail to the Falklands along with HMS *Tyne* and exercise British sovereignty. Mestivier sailed for the Falklands in December 1832 aboard the *Sarandia*. When he arrived, there was a mutiny and he was murdered. José Maria de Pinedo, the *Sarandia*'s captain, attempted to restore order to the colony.

It was at this rather confused juncture that HMS *Clio* sailed into the harbour, hoisted the Union Jack and hauled down the Buenos Aires flag, which was returned to Captain Pinedo. The Argentine garrison was ordered to leave and sailed out of Puerto Soledad on 4 January 1833. From that moment onward the Falkland Islands were to remain in continuous British possession until April 1982.

Argentina protested vigorously against Britain's action. Indeed, Argentina continued to contest at more or less regular intervals the British occupation of the Falklands, although there was a long period, between 1849 and 1884, during which little or no protest was made. Britain largely ignored the remonstrations, asserting that the question of sovereignty was settled. Palmerston said that the matter should simply be dropped. In 1884, Argentina asked for the dispute to be submitted to international arbitration, but Britain declined to respond to the suggestion. Renewed protests at the beginning of the twentieth century prompted the Foreign Office to instruct the Assistant Librarian, Gaston de Bernhardt, to prepare a memorandum on the question, and this was duly presented in 1910.

Contrary to received Foreign Office wisdom at the time, de Bernhardt's memorandum suggested that the foundation of Britain's claim, that sovereignty of the Falkland Islands lay unquestionably with Britain in 1833, was perhaps less solid than had previously been thought. In a book published in 1927, *The Struggle for the Falkland Islands,* an American academic called Julius Goebel concluded that Argentina's claims were based on much firmer ground than Britain's, although he conceded that in fine the question depended more on power than on abstract legal reasoning. The Foreign Office publicly suggested that the conclusion was motivated more by American hostility to perceived British colonialism than purely academic research. In any case, as the British Ambassador in Buenos Aires, Sir Malcolm Robertson, put it, nobody seriously expected Britain to evacuate the islands. During this period Argentina made various attempts to assert its claim in a variety of ways (according to a strategy referred to by the Foreign Office as a 'policy of pin-pricks'), for example printing maps or issuing postage stamps showing the Malvinas as Argentine territory. But the Foreign Office found indications that the Argentine authorities may have at least tacitly recognised British sovereignty over the Falkland Islands, when, for example, in 1967 it received an Identity Card signed by the Buenos Aires chief of police in 1920, indicating the place of birth of the holder as 'provincia de: *Islas Malvinas,* nación: *Inglaterra'.*

By 1933, a hundred years after Britain's annexation of the islands, the Foreign Office was beginning to rely more on the length of continuous peaceful occupation to justify British sovereignty than on sovereignty rights as they stood in 1833. Anthony Eden wrote in 1936 that such a period of possession, irrespective of whether it was disputed or not, ought to provide a sufficiently sound title in law. This title by 'prescription' grew stronger with every year that went by.

The head of the American Department in the Foreign Office, John Troutbeck, was however still worried about Britain's claim, and wrote that, 'the difficulty of the position is that our seizure of the Falkland Islands in 1833 was so arbitrary a procedure as judged by the ideology of the present day. It is therefore not easy to explain our possession without showing ourselves up as international bandits'. His view was not shared by more robust spirits in the Foreign Office who rejected it as 'unnecessarily apologetic'.

Argentina promoted the argument of geographical proximity, claiming that the Falkland Islands were located on part of Argentina's continental shelf. Against that it has been pointed out that the islands are some 300 miles from the mainland of South America.

The Falkland Island dependencies have, on occasions, been added to Argentine claims. The group, which includes South Georgia (San Pedro to the

Argentines) and the South Sandwich Islands, were annexed by the United Kingdom in the late nineteenth century on the grounds of discovery. Britain has always stressed that while the dependencies are, for reasons of convenience, administered from the Falkland Islands, they remain separate territories directly dependent on the United Kingdom. Finally, Britain's Antarctic territories are not connected with – at least not directly – the dispute over the Falkland Islands. There are overlapping Argentine, British and Chilean claims in the Antarctic, but sovereignty over Antarctica was frozen for a period of thirty years under the Antarctic Treaty of 1959 which came into effect in 1961. The moratorium was renewed for a further thirty years in 1991.

The only conclusion that can be drawn from this brief summary of the background to the sovereignty dispute is that it is an inordinately complicated affair. It is perhaps almost irreconcilable. To a certain extent the argument is academic, not only because of the unambiguous desire of the Falkland Islands' population to remain under British administration but also because, however complex the issue, the existence of a sovereignty dispute could provide no legal justification for Argentina's invasion of the islands in 1982.

THREE

From the Second World War to 1982

During the Second World War there were fears that pro-Nazi elements in Argentina might take advantage of the situation to occupy the islands. A garrison of some 1,500 men defended them. It has been claimed that the Argentine Government gave orders for a plan to occupy the islands to be made ready, and indeed that an invasion was ordered in 1945, only to be called off after the Allied victory. There has also been a suggestion that Britain might have been considering transferring sovereignty to Argentina in 1940, although this is based simply on the title of a file held in the Public Record Office which has not yet been made public.

After the Second World War Argentina, under the Presidency of Juan Perón, enthusiastically took up the dispute. A 'Malvinas Day' was declared and there were rousing proclamations, but no attempt was made to use force. In 1955 Britain tried to bring the question of sovereignty over the Falkland Island dependencies, which were disputed by Argentina, to the International Court of Justice (as well as Chilean claims over the British Antarctic Territories) but neither Argentina nor Chile agreed to such arbitration.

In 1960 the United Nations General Assembly solemnly proclaimed, in Resolution 1514 (XV), 'the necessity of bringing to a speedy and unconditional end colonialism in all its forms and manifestations'. While it recalled the right of all peoples to self-determination it also stated its conviction that all peoples have 'an inalienable right to complete freedom, the exercise of their sovereignty and the integrity of their national territory'. Argentina claimed that the British administration of the Falkland Islands was an affront to their territorial integrity. They raised the matter with the Committee of 24 which was charged with implementing the policy of granting independence to colonial countries and peoples. In 1965, after persistent Argentine lobbying, another resolution of the General Assembly, Resolution 2065, recalling Resolution 1514, considered that the Falkland Islands (Malvinas) were an instance of colonialism, and invited the governments of the United Kingdom and Argentina to initiate negotiations with a view to achieving a peaceful settlement of the dispute, consistent with the principle of granting independence to colonial countries and peoples and 'bearing in mind the interests of the population of the Falkland Islands'.

Britain argued that the Falkland Islands did not constitute a colonial possession in the usual understanding of the term. The people of the islands were not deprived of their political rights or otherwise oppressed by a foreign colonial power. On the contrary, the Falklanders did everything they could to remain under British administration. Britain increasingly pointed to the concept of self-determination, and argued that this applied to the Falkland islanders. It noted the repeated expressions of the islanders' wish to remain British. The Argentines challenged the application of the concept of self-determination, claiming that the population was in reality a settler population and pointing out that the authorities on the Falkland Islands had made it difficult for Argentines to settle there. But the issue of the Falkland Islands remained 'peripheral' and the United Kingdom's Permanent Representative to the United Nations in 1982, Sir Anthony Parsons, said that he did not remember anyone having spoken to him about the subject before April 1982.

Alongside these diplomatic manoeuvres, a number of individual actions took place in the 1960s, most notably an attempted 'liberation' carried out in 1966 by a group of men who hi-jacked a plane and forced it to land at Stanley airfield. The Argentine Government officially frowned on such initiatives and preferred to pursue a negotiated settlement.

Britain did give effect to Resolution 2065 and began talks with Buenos Aires. Negotiations seemed to be progressing in Argentina's direction, especially while George Brown was Foreign Secretary. Discussions with Argentina produced a Memorandum of Understanding, agreed at official level in August 1968, to the effect that Britain was prepared to include the sovereignty question in talks with Argentina provided the islanders' wishes were respected. The British Government was subjected to intense pressure from, among others, the newly formed Falkland Island Committee, who insisted that the Falklanders would have to agree to the proposals, and Lord Chalfont was sent to discuss the question with the population. He was left in no doubt that the islanders would not approve the memorandum, and debate in the House of Commons effectively put an end to any proposed solution which did not explicitly meet their approval. The Government pledged that the islanders' wishes would be 'paramount'.

In response to this situation, a policy emerged whereby Buenos Aires would try to win the hearts and minds of the islanders and generally seek to persuade the Falklanders of the advantages of closer association with Argentina. In 1971 a 'Communications Agreement' was signed, under which Falkland islanders would be free to travel to Argentina, direct air and sea links would be set up, and post and telephone rates would be harmonised. In 1974 Argentina agreed to supply fuel to the islands at mainland rates. It was only when this policy seemed to be getting nowhere that the threat of more direct action became apparent. The Government racked its brains to find ways of getting round the impasse. One idea that emerged was that economic co-operation might encourage closer links, and it was apparently with this aim in mind that in 1975 the Government commissioned a survey under the direction of Lord Shackleton. The Argentines, however, feared that the survey was intended to establish ways in which Britain might develop and reinforce its sovereignty over the islands and protested vehemently. In February 1976 an Argentine naval vessel fired across the bows of the Royal Research Ship *Shackleton*. Another Argentine action at this time was the secret establishment during the summer of 1976 of a scientific base on the island of Southern Thule in the South Sandwich Islands. When Britain found out, the Government decided to do nothing, and indeed Parliament was not even informed of the fact until 1978.

In November 1977, amid growing tension, the Government sent a nuclear-powered submarine and two frigates to the region, just in case. The deployment was kept secret, but the Prime Minister, James Callaghan, later said that he had told Maurice Oldfield, the head of MI6, and intimated that he would not be displeased if the Argentines found out. Callaghan was under the impression that the message had indeed been conveyed, discreetly, although there is no documentary evidence that it actually was. This deployment was not made public until 30 March 1982, when Argentina had already launched the invasion force that precipitated the Falklands War.

It was recognised that unless the momentum of talks with Argentina was sustained, there was a real risk that Buenos Aires might tilt in favour of a military solution. Consequently, although Britain did not wish to discuss sovereignty, it did agree to discuss 'hypothetical changes to the constitutional arrangements' concerning the territory. Various 'solutions' were considered, including the idea of 'leaseback', whereby nominal sovereignty would be given to Argentina, while British administration would be maintained for a fixed number of years until the final hand-over. This idea worried many British officials, because it suggested that Britain might be prepared to hand over a population that wished to remain British to a regime which at that time was particularly unappealing. Argentina's human-rights record was very poor, especially in the wake of the military coup of 1976, with the armed forces conducting a 'dirty war' against alleged insurrectionist elements, kidnapping, torturing and murdering political opponents. Thousands of people were simply taken away and killed. They became known collectively as the '*desaparecidos*', the disappeared.

In July 1979, shortly after the establishment of a Conservative government under Margaret Thatcher, the Foreign and Commonwealth Secretary, Lord Carrington, sent Nicholas Ridley, Minister of State at the Foreign and Commonwealth Office, to visit the islands. In the discussions following the visit, Carrington defined three possible policies. The first, a commitment to maintain a sufficiently powerful force on the islands to oppose any attempted invasion, known as the 'Fortress Falklands' policy, was ruled out as excessively expensive, especially against a background of increasing pressure on the defence budget. The second was a 'sovereignty freeze' accompanied by negotiations on various peripheral issues. There was, however, little prospect of long-term Argentine patience if this policy was adopted.

The third idea was to enter negotiations with a genuine willingness to consider ways of solving the sovereignty problem. The most attractive option in this third policy, which Carrington thought 'might, just might be negotiated with Argentina and become acceptable to the islanders', was leaseback. He knew that the islanders were not keen, but felt that it was worth a try. But the Prime Minister did not want to take the matter any further until other more pressing matters, such as the future of Rhodesia, had been settled. The Joint Intelligence Committee judged if Argentina thought it was getting nowhere with diplomacy, it might resort to force, but felt overall that the danger was not as great as it had been.

In July 1980 the Cabinet Defence Committee authorised Carrington to try and reach a solution on the basis of leaseback. Ridley made a second visit to the islands in November 1980. He found that a substantial minority was against leaseback, but that the majority had not yet made up its mind. On his return, Ridley made a statement on the question to the House of Commons, but was given a hostile reception from MPs on both sides of the House. Labour MPs protested against any attempt to pressure the islanders into an agreement with an unsavoury military regime such as Argentina, while Conservative backbenchers regretted that the question of sovereignty had been raised at all, as, they suggested, this could only weaken Britain's claim. In the face of such opposition, the Government re-affirmed the 'paramountcy' of the islanders' wishes. The result was something of an impasse.

Carrington recognised that the situation was dangerous, and that military action could no longer be discounted. Advice from the intelligence services, however, consistently predicted that if there was such a response, it would take the form of a gradual escalation. Moreover, the Falkland Islands Joint Councils agreed in early January 1981 that further talks should be held with Argentina, at which representatives of the islanders would be present and should press for a sovereignty freeze. The talks began in February 1981 in New York, and the sovereignty freeze was predictably rejected, but at least negotiations were continuing. Argentine patience, however, was beginning to run short.

In July 1981 the Joint Intelligence Committee updated its assessment of the situation. It felt that the most likely Argentine response to lack of progress would be to escalate the dispute through diplomatic and economic measures, such as disrupting the transport links, food and oil supplies or medical aid arrangements, or through occupation of an uninhabited part of the dependencies along the

1976 Southern Thule model. If Argentina thought there was no prospect of eventual transfer of sovereignty, it might take military action, swiftly and without warning, and this could go as far as a full-scale invasion of the Falkland Islands.

In a report sent to Carrington in July 1981, Ridley advised that leaseback remained the only feasible policy, and recommended an education campaign to persuade the islanders that this was the best solution. Carrington declined to take any action that would be interpreted as putting pressure on the islanders and might therefore be counter-productive. When the British Ambassador in Buenos Aires learned about this, he protested strongly, suggesting that there was now 'no strategy at all beyond a general Micawberism'. In October 1981 prospects of a change of heart among the islanders were further dented with the election of a new Legislative Council reflecting increased resistance to any proposals for a transfer of sovereignty, either through leaseback or any other way. However, it did agree to continue talks.

At the same time as the room for manoeuvre enjoyed by the diplomats in the Foreign Office was being reduced, Britain's resolve to keep a firm hand on its South Atlantic possessions seemed to be diminishing. The 1981 British Nationality Act meant that a number of Falkland islanders would be deprived of full rights as British citizens. There were plans for cuts in the budget of the British Antarctic Survey, and especially proposals for the withdrawal of its scientific base at Grytviken in South Georgia, although funds were in fact found and the base was able to continue its work. Above all, the controversial 1981 Defence Review had planned for drastic cuts in defence spending, especially affecting the Navy, including the withdrawal of the only permanent naval presence in the South Atlantic, the ice-breaking patrol ship HMS *Endurance*, by 15 April 1982. (This was confirmed in the House of Lords on 30 June 1981.) Carrington wrote three times to the Secretary of State for Defence responsible for the cuts, John Nott, to ask him to give *Endurance* a reprieve, but this was refused.

Argentina watched closely as Britain seemed to be announcing in effect that it was no longer prepared to maintain even a token naval presence and at the same time was apparently weakening its links with the population. The inference apparently drawn from these observations was that the Government was not really interested in the Falkland Islands, but was prevented by a vociferous lobby in Parliament and the resolute distrust expressed by the islanders from suggesting any move towards a transfer of sovereignty to Argentina.

It therefore may have seemed to some of Argentina's leaders that Britain could be pushed into accepting a solution that would otherwise be too politically sensitive. The very dangerous view emerged that while Britain would protest vehemently against any military occupation, it would not be prepared to do anything more than gesticulate.

Argentina also took comfort from the new friendship between Argentina and the United States. Under President Carter, the United States had been distinctly cool towards Buenos Aires because of the latter's poor human-rights record. The Reagan administration saw Argentina as a bulwark against communism, especially in so far as it could help the United States deal with the Sandinistas in Nicaragua. The Argentines were also aware of Washington's instinctive hostility to any suggestion of colonialism. All of these factors led the Argentine junta to conclude that the United States would not support Britain, and that this made British military intervention to protect or re-conquer the Falklands even less likely.

CROSS-PURPOSES: OPERATION ALFA AND
OPERATION AZUL

In Argentina pressure for a rapid solution to the question of the Malvinas increased when on

22 December 1981 General Galtieri took power at the head of a military junta comprising himself as commander-in-chief of the Army, Admiral Anaya in charge of the Navy and Brigadier Lami Dozo of the Air Force. Admiral Anaya was known to have hard-line views on the 'recovery' of the islands, and it is believed that he was persuaded to give his support to Galtieri on condition that the junta would give priority to this objective. There were other reasons why the Malvinas became increasingly significant at this time. The 150th anniversary of Britain's annexation of the Falkland Islands was due in January 1983. More importantly, the junta was finding it difficult to deal with increasingly hostile public opinion. The military government had taken power ostensibly to redress Argentina's ailing economy, but by late 1981 the economic situation was deteriorating sharply. The armed forces' role in the 'dirty war' was being more and more openly contested. Finally, Argentina's foreign policy had suffered a setback when arbitration in connection with its territorial dispute with Chile went in favour of the latter. The 'crusade' to retrieve the Falklands was about the only policy still viable that would unite Argentine public opinion.

Almost immediately the junta under Galtieri assumed office plans were set in train to prepare an armed invasion. At the same time the diplomatic initiative was to be stepped up, with pressure being put on Britain to accelerate the pace of negotiations. The junta hoped to achieve its objective by January 1983. This was not the first time plans to occupy the Falklands had been made, and indeed in the Argentine armed forces such plans were almost a tradition. It was stressed that any such occupation would have to be bloodless, so as to preserve international opinion. This meant that secrecy was essential and only a handful of people knew anything about them. The reports were hand-written to reduce the risk of leaks. The junta remained firmly convinced that Britain would protest but stop short of military action, so much so that it did not even make any contingency arrangements to prepare for a possible British military response. Indeed, it was intended that once the islands had been occupied the garrison would be substantially reduced.

Plans to challenge Britain's hold in the South Atlantic had also been prepared by the previous military government under Admiral Viola, and one of them seems to have continued under its own momentum, perhaps driven by more hawkish elements in the Argentine Navy who were unaware of – or chose to ignore – the planning process set up by Galtieri. This scheme, Operation Alfa, sought to establish an Argentine presence on the island of South Georgia, similar, although more ambitious, to the scientific base on Southern Thule. This was based on a contract signed by an Argentine businessman called Constantine Davidoff to recover scrap metal from the old whaling installations at Leith. The contract was a genuine commercial venture, and there is no evidence that Davidoff knew that he was being used by the armed forces (although there is no evidence to the contrary either). The Argentine Navy offered to help him, especially as regards transport to the islands. The Government also gave Davidoff various tax concessions which made the contract an attractive one. Operation Alfa was entirely in the hands of the Navy.

Meanwhile, the central planning work group concluded that the operation to recover the archipelago, Operation Azul, was feasible and acceptable and that the Argentine armed forces would be ready to carry out the operation from 15 May 1982 at the earliest, although the preferred date was 9 July, a national holiday in Argentina. By that time several factors would be working in Argentina's favour: HMS *Endurance* would have been withdrawn; the Arctic winter would be drawing in, and the increasingly severe conditions of the South Atlantic would make any British military response impossible. Moreover, Argentina would have received most of the military materiel it had ordered. The planning group stressed that if the element of surprise were lost, with the likelihood that Britain would reinforce the islands, then the operation would be compromised. Operation Alfa could thus imperil Operation Azul, and so orders were given for Alfa to be stopped. They were apparently ignored.

The over-arching need for secrecy also confused Argentina's diplomatic position. Talks conducted by Enrique Ros, Argentina's Deputy Foreign Minister, with his British counterparts were, according to Foreign Office Minister Richard Luce, constructive, and after the meetings in New York a very positive statement was agreed. A joint communiqué published on 1 March 1982 stated that, 'the meeting took place in a cordial and positive spirit' and that the two governments 'reaffirmed their resolve to find a solution to the sovereignty dispute'. This was not at all what the junta wanted, and a more threatening statement was issued shortly afterwards by Nicanor Costa Mendez, Argentina's new Foreign Minister, expressing Argentine hopes that the new diplomatic initiative would lead to an early solution to the dispute. 'However,' the statement concluded, 'should this not occur, Argentina reserves the right to terminate the working of this mechanism and to choose freely the procedure which best accords with her interests.'

FOUR

The Falklands War

On 20 December 1981 Davidoff landed without
permission at Leith on the island of South Georgia
on board the ice-breaker *Almirante Irizar* to survey the
whaling station. The landing was reported by a
French yacht that happened to be in the vicinity.
When the British Antarctic Survey base commander
from Grytviken, some 15 miles away, reached the
harbour he found the Argentines had gone, but had
left a chalked message claiming that the island
belonged to Argentina. Davidoff later called at the
British Embassy in Buenos Aires to apologise and
inform them that he would soon be returning. He
was told that he should first report to Grytviken and
follow the normal procedure for entry. On 9 March
1982 Davidoff notified the British Embassy in Buenos
Aires that a group of workmen would be leaving for

South Georgia just two days later on the *Bahia Buen Suceso*. When the *Bahia Buen Suceso* reached South Georgia on 19 March it sailed directly to Leith and failed to report to Grytviken, contrary to the regulations that had been explained to Davidoff via his lawyer and which, in any case, as the Falkland Islands Governor Rex Hunt recalls in his autobiography, were well known to the captain.

Scientists from the British Antarctic Survey observed a large group of men at Leith, and noted that the Argentine flag was flying above the manager's house. The scientists informed the captain of the ship that the men had entered South Georgia illegally. Hunt gave orders that the Argentines were to return to their ship and report immediately to the authorities at Grytviken. He also informed London. The Foreign and Commonwealth Office instructed the Embassy in Buenos Aires to tell the Argentine Foreign Ministry that they were taking the affair seriously, and that if the men did not comply with the instructions Britain would be forced to take action.

HMS *Endurance* was given orders to go to South Georgia with a group of twenty-two Marines and its Wasp helicopters. In the Falklands, where these developments were being closely followed, someone had entered the offices of the Argentine air service LADE and written on the top of the desk (in toothpaste!) 'tit for tat, you buggers'. The Argentine press expressed outrage at this incident and it is clear that the Argentine armed forces shared this reaction, at least officially.

The *Bahia Buen Suceso* left the harbour on 21 March, but observers reported that a group of men remained. The Argentine authorities were informed that *Endurance* was sailing to Leith to remove the party. But after Costa Mendez had made representations to the British Embassy suggesting that to remove the men by force would only be playing into the hands of the hard-liners, *Endurance* was ordered to go to Grytviken and wait for further orders. A message was sent by Carrington to Costa Mendez agreeing that the Argentine authorities should take the men off South Georgia. If they did not, Britain would have to remove them. On 25 March the *Bahia Paraiso* arrived in Leith, but far from removing the men, began to unload further stores. In Argentina, Costa Mendez announced at a press conference that the men would be given protection.

INVASION

Fearing that Britain was about to reinforce the military defence of the Falkland Islands, the junta decided to launch Operation Azul before it was too late. Argentina's invasion force left port on 28 March with orders to occupy the Falkland Islands on 1 April. Reports published on 30 March in the *Daily Telegraph* to the effect that a nuclear-powered submarine, HMS *Superb*, was already on its way south convinced the junta that they had to proceed with the operation without delay. Because of bad weather the invasion was postponed until 2 April. Intelligence suggesting that a military occupation was imminent was passed to London on 31 March. The Governor was informed, but told that he should not take any action that would compromise the last-minute efforts then being made to persuade the junta to back down. On 29 March, a fresh detachment of Marines had arrived from Montevideo, not on HMS *Endurance*, which was busy with the South Georgia incident, but on a research ship, the *John Briscoe*. They joined the twenty-six men from the previous party still on the Falklands. The senior officer of the new group was to begin his command on 1 April 1982.

During the evening of 31 March Prime Minister Thatcher was discussing the Falklands situation in the House of Commons with a small group of ministers and advisers when Admiral Sir Henry Leach, the First Sea Lord and Chief of the Naval Staff, arrived. Leach had fought Nott's defence cuts vigorously and now had an opportunity to show the value of the Navy. He advised the Prime Minister that the armed forces could mount a successful operation to recover the islands if necessary. Indeed, he told her he thought they should do so because if they did not Britain's standing would be diminished. He was told to make the appropriate preparations.

Thatcher asked President Reagan to intercede directly with Galtieri. When he attempted to do so, on the evening of 1 April, he was at first unable to contact Galtieri, being told that he was unavailable. When Galtieri did take the call he was non-committal and made no undertaking to refrain from using force. It was already too late.

The Governor told the Marines to prepare to resist occupation and made arrangements to intern the Argentines on the island as soon as he received definite information that the invasion was really going to happen. Meanwhile, Sir Anthony Parsons began making his own preparations to obtain on 1 April an appeal for restraint from the President of the Security Council and later a resolution calling on the Argentines to withdraw. The Governor was finally given definite confirmation of the impending invasion at 3.30 p.m. Falklands time (three hours behind GMT) on 1 April. The telegram said: 'We have apparently reliable evidence that an Argentine task force will gather off Cape Pembroke early tomorrow morning, 2 April. You will wish to make your dispositions accordingly.' The Governor's communications officer regretted that the telegram had not at least wished them luck . . .

The Argentine invasion group arrived in the early hours of the morning of 2 April. The Argentines on the Falklands had by then been rounded up and interned. The Marines had left their barracks and deployed to various defensive positions, particularly at Government House in Port Stanley. They had selected what they thought was the most likely beach for a landing and set up some defences there, but the Argentines chose to disembark elsewhere. A small group of Marines attacked an armed personnel carrier on the road towards Stanley and brought it to a standstill. Meanwhile, at Government House, a fierce exchange of gunfire left one Argentine officer dying in the grounds and several others injured. The Governor, armed with a pistol, took shelter under a solid oak table.

A cease-fire was proposed. The Governor asked the commanding officer of the Royal Marines what the situation was, and he was told that the Argentines had heavy weapons which could be brought to bear on Government House and yet remain out of range of any weapons possessed by the defenders. When he spoke to the Argentine commanding officer he ordered him and all his men to leave forthwith, a demand that the Argentine declined to obey, pointing out that he had a much superior force and that resistance was useless. Hunt had to accept that that was indeed the case, and ordered the Marines to surrender. They were taken prisoner and later flown out to Montevideo. The Governor and a number of Falklanders were also expelled from the islands. The Argentine authorities said that they would ensure that there was no ill-treatment of the Falklanders. Some of the Argentine servicemen have said that they were surprised to find that the population of the Malvinas spoke English and did not welcome them as liberators.

In the United Kingdom there was some considerable confusion about what exactly was going on in the South Atlantic. News was filtering through from Buenos Aires that the Malvinas had been seized. At 11 a.m. London time on Friday 2 April the Deputy Foreign Minister Humphrey Atkins told the House of Commons that, contrary to the news reports from Argentina and persistent rumours, he had no evidence that an invasion had taken place and that the Government had been in contact with Hunt less than an hour before. It later turned out that he was mistaken. At 2.30 p.m., the Leader of the House of Commons, Francis Pym, stated that there had been no confirmation of any change in the situation. It was not until 6 p.m. that an official announcement was made at a press conference at the Foreign Office.

This confusion only made things worse for the Government. It looked as if it had not only been caught unprepared but was also unable to establish what was going on. Confirmation of the invasion was given in time for the newspapers to prepare news and comment for their Saturday morning editions. The House of Commons was recalled for an emergency debate on the Saturday morning, the first time this had happened since the Suez crisis – an inauspicious precedent. The Government was in trouble, and Thatcher was well aware of the danger. Her declaration to the House of Commons was restrained in tone, in contrast to the excited atmosphere on the benches both behind and opposite her.

The Prime Minister told the Commons that the Falklands were British territory and that the Government's objective was to free the islands from occupation and return them to British administration as soon as possible. A number of MPs asked 'How?' Thatcher then briefly summarised the history of the dispute and announced that a task force was already being assembled and would shortly be leaving for the South Atlantic. Some ships were indeed already at sea. Diplomatic efforts would be pursued and the

United Nations Security Council had met the previous day and would continue its talks.

The mood of the House that morning was such that the Prime Minister's reference to the United Nations provoked laughter, and she had to remind Labour MPs that if the Government had not requested a meeting of the Security Council they would have been the first to demand one. Emotions were running high. Michael Foot, leader of the Labour Party, declared that Britain had 'a moral duty, a political duty and every other kind of duty' to ensure that the people of the Falkland Islands could continue to live, as they wished, on the basis of association with Britain. The back-bencher Edward du Cann would make no allowances for the difficulties involved in sending a force to the area, referring to historical disdain for logistical differences, and saying that he did not remember the Duke of Wellington 'whining about Torres Vedras'. Perhaps the most celebrated remark was made by Enoch Powell, who recalled that the Prime Minister had been referred to as the 'Iron Lady', and challenged her to live up to this sobriquet.

There were echoes of 1940: Sir Nigel Fisher, a Conservative MP, perhaps unwisely, referred to the fact that Britain had been 'pre-empted' just as it had been in 1940, and recalled that this had led to the fall of the Chamberlain government. The Labour MP Edward Rowlands asked how it was that the Government had not seen fit to take action to counter the invasion, and concluded that the 'guilty men' should not go free. Patrick Cormack, a Conservative MP, congratulated the leader of the Opposition, saying that he 'truly spoke for Britain', again recalling words used forty-two years earlier, and, in a vitriolic attack on the Foreign Office, Labour's Douglas Jay accused it of 'appeasement'.

The response to the Falklands crisis in the House of Commons meant that the ensuing conflict was at least as much Parliament's war as it was Thatcher's, a point made forcefully by Hugo Young in *One of Us*. The Government knew that it would stand or fall by its ability to retrieve the situation to the satisfaction of Parliament. It could have no illusions about the reception it would get if it agreed to terms which fell short of the principle that the wishes of the islanders should remain paramount. To a very large extent, therefore, the Government's hands were tied, and it had no choice but to take up the challenge.

Also on 3 April Argentine forces attacked South Georgia. The small Marine detachment put up a spirited resistance and shot down a helicopter. It severely damaged the Argentine ship *Guerrico* with a combination of small arms and anti-tank rockets but later surrendered as the situation was hopeless.

In Britain, the powerful thirst for ministerial blood was satisfied with the resignation on Monday 5 April of Carrington, Atkins and Luce. Carrington said that he did not in fact believe that the Foreign Office had done the wrong thing, given the advice they had had, but recognised that there had been a national humiliation and that as the minister responsible he should stand down. He had not heard the debate in the Commons – he had taken part in a less heated debate in the Lords – and had not, for instance, heard Sir Bernard Braine talk about 'weasel words from successive Foreign Office Ministers'. He was, however, shaken by angry criticism from the Conservative backbenchers at a meeting held shortly after the debate. This was compounded by newspaper comment, especially from *The Times* on Monday 5 April in its monumental editorial 'We are All Falklanders Now', and he wrote to the Prime Minister tendering his resignation that same day. He was replaced by Francis Pym, who had been Foreign Secretary in Opposition and was a former Chief Whip. Pym's steady style reassured the Conservative MPs. Thatcher had her reservations about him, however, and wrote in her autobiography that his appointment 'heralded serious difficulties for the conduct of the campaign itself'.

Nott also offered to resign, and indeed it was argued in some quarters that, because of his role in implementing the defence cuts and particularly for insisting on the withdrawal of HMS *Endurance*, he should have gone, but Thatcher insisted that he should stay. Nott had in fact made it clear even before the Falklands crisis that he had no intention of remaining in politics for very long, and left the government and the House of Commons in 1983.

In Buenos Aires the situation was both entirely different and remarkably similar. It was entirely different in that Argentine public opinion was almost hysterical in its joy at the news of the 'recovery' of the Malvinas, and workers who, only days before, had taken part in hostile demonstrations against the junta declared their unswerving support. For many it was a highly emotional, even religious, experience. The situation was remarkably similar to that in the United Kingdom in that the junta knew that it would stand or fall on its ability to retain the islands. Its policy of resorting to military occupation merely to hasten the pace of negotiations was made impossible by the rapturous enthusiasm of the crowds. Its hands, then, were also firmly tied.

Meanwhile, Britain had already scored a major diplomatic triumph. Parsons had succeeded in achieving an overwhelming vote in the Security

Council for the draft he had prepared and which, on 3 April 1982, became Security Council Resolution 502. This called for an immediate cessation of hostilities, withdrawal of Argentine forces and diplomatic action for a negotiated settlement. Britain maintained that if diplomacy failed, it still had a right under article 51 of the United Nations charter to take appropriate military action in self-defence: 'Nothing in the present Charter shall impair the inherent right of individual or collective self-defense if an armed attack occurs against a Member of the United Nations, until the Security Council has taken measures necessary to maintain international peace and security.'

In Argentina General Mario Benjamin Menéndez was appointed military governor of the Malvinas and arrived there on 3 April. The Argentines promised that the islanders would be allowed to continue to live according to their own customs, but various changes were gradually imposed, beginning with driving on the right.

TASK FORCE

The task force sent to the South Atlantic to carry out Operation Corporate, as the campaign to recover the islands was named, was a huge enterprise, involving in all over 110 ships (Royal Navy, Royal Maritime Auxiliary Service, Royal Fleet Auxiliary and ships taken up from trade) and some 28,000 men. Some of the ships were taking part in exercises in the Mediterranean when the crisis broke, and were sent directly southwards. Others, including the aircraft carriers HMS *Hermes* and HMS *Invincible*, left Portsmouth amid great publicity on 5 April. More ships left Portsmouth and other British ports, including Gibraltar, throughout April and May, with varying degrees of publicity. The general perception of this display of naval might was that it would persuade the Argentincs to negotiate before the force reached the islands. But the ships had to be placed on a war footing in case the diplomacy did not work. The logistics of the operation were daunting. Indeed, loading of the big ships that left Britain on 5 April had not been finished, and helicopters continued carrying supplies to the flotilla as it made its way down the English Channel towards the Atlantic. The speed with which the task force was assembled also created difficulties for the few journalists who had been able to secure accreditation to accompany the ships southwards; many of them had to make a mad dash to the ports to get there in time.

The United States immediately offered Britain the use of its Wideawake base on the island of Ascension.

Ascension was British territory, and under the terms of the lease to the United States Britain could use it in an emergency. Ascension provided an invaluable staging-post, where hurriedly stowed equipment and supplies could be re-organised in the correct battle order and any missing supplies brought in by air. The RAF began a series of transport flights which at one stage meant that Ascension's airstrip became among the busiest in the world. America secretly supplied aviation fuel and weapons, including the vital new Sidewinder air-to-air missile for Britain's Harrier jets, and helped with intelligence and communications.

Officially, the United States was neutral. Reagan explained that he was troubled by this dispute between two friendly countries, and he hoped that bloodshed could be avoided. It was a dispute that he had some difficulty understanding, remarking that it seemed to be a quarrel over some very remote territory. He was keen to avoid having to choose between his closest ally in Europe and his most valued partner in the struggle against Marxism in Latin America, and so he charged his Secretary of State, General Alexander Haig, with the difficult task of brokering a diplomatic settlement. For the next three weeks or so Haig spent most of his time flying between Washington, London and Buenos Aires. Within the United States opinion seemed to some extent to be divided between those, most notably

Jeane Kirkpatrick, US Representative at the United
Nations, who had been most assiduous in developing
co-operation with South America and were worried
about the effect of the crisis on the United States'
foreign affairs in its own hemisphere, and the
'Europeans', like General Haig and particularly Caspar
Weinberger, the US Secretary of Defense, who felt
closer ties with the United Kingdom were appropriate
as part of the Anglo-American 'special relationship'.

Britain's European partners announced an embargo
on arms sales to Argentina, as well as economic
sanctions, although, as the conflict progressed, support
for European economic sanctions declined when
Ireland and Italy withdrew. Britain received clear
messages of support from many heads of state, perhaps
most notably and most rapidly from President
Mitterrand of France.

The main diplomatic effort, however, remained
firmly in the hands of General Haig. It proved to be
an extraordinarily difficult mission, and ultimately
cost him his job. He began his shuttle diplomacy on
8 April in London, where he was able to gauge the
Prime Minister's determination. He gave her his
assurance that there would be no repeat of the Suez
crisis of 1956 – the United States would not force
Britain to back down. Haig floated various
proposals for mutual withdrawal and an interim

administration, but Thatcher told him they were too 'woolly'. He flew to Buenos Aires on 9 April, where huge crowds were assembled to show the strength of public support for the junta's move. Haig realised that it was going to be a difficult undertaking, but felt that the stakes were so high that he had to try.

Haig found negotiations with the junta extremely difficult. It was clear to him that the Air Force was less enthusiastic than the Navy, with the Army somewhere in between. He believed that had Galtieri been acting alone he might have been able to accept a compromise. But Haig soon realised that every step in the process had to be agreed by a large number of high-ranking officers in all three branches of the armed services. Galtieri also took great pleasure in addressing the crowds massed in the square in front of the Casa Rosada, Argentina's presidential palace, and found himself promising a stronger line than he had perhaps intended.

Haig found the junta reluctant to accept anything short of a commitment to begin negotiations with a guarantee that Argentina would ultimately be granted sovereignty. He was, nevertheless, able to obtain some concessions from the junta, and returned to his plane on 11 April to fly to London with at least some hope that progress could be made. As he was getting on the plane, however, Costa Mendez handed him a paper outlining some further thoughts on the negotiations. The message was a retreat from everything that had been painstakingly agreed the previous evening. It stated that Argentina would only agree to withdrawal, partial or otherwise, if there was a prior undertaking that sovereignty would be transferred to Argentina by the end of the year. 'This', said Haig, 'was a formula for war'.

When Haig arrived in London he discussed the proposals with Thatcher and the War Cabinet. He also spoke with Costa Mendez on the telephone. He then flew with his team to Washington for a rest, and then on to Buenos Aires again, arriving on 15 April. He had a proposal to submit to the junta, which had been approved by Thatcher, according to which the Argentines would withdraw from the islands and the British task force stop 1,000 miles from the islands; an interim administration would be formed with Britain, Argentina and the United States; sanctions would be lifted, and negotiations set in train with a view to achieving a solution by December 1982. Haig says he thought the terms were impossible to refuse, but the Argentines rejected them. Once again, they wanted an assurance that the final outcome would be sovereignty for Argentina. They also demanded the right for Argentine citizens to

47

settle freely on the islands. Haig asked to meet the junta to explain what the consequences would be. He spoke with Galtieri, who seemed keen to reach a negotiated solution. The following day, 17 April, Haig attended a meeting with the full junta. Talks continued all next day, and by the early hours of 19 April a package was agreed, although Haig told the Argentines he thought it would be difficult for the British to accept. Further modifications were introduced that morning to try and meet some of the expected objections.

As Haig was about to leave, the Foreign Minister again met him at the airport, and again handed him a letter to read on the plane. A no doubt dejected Haig noted that, once again, the message represented a move back to the original hard-line demands. The Argentines insisted they would have to have a promise that sovereignty would be transferred to Argentina by 31 December 1982.

Meanwhile, the task force continued its route towards the South Atlantic, using its time at sea to prepare for war. Weapons were tested, men were kept fit. On 12 April, a maritime exclusion zone was announced. A detachment of ships, including HMS *Antrim*, HMS *Tidespring* and HMS *Plymouth*, with special forces and Royal Marines embarked, was ordered to proceed with all speed to South

Georgia. HMS *Endurance* joined the group on 14 April.

SOUTH GEORGIA, OR A DISASTER ONLY NARROWLY AVERTED

Plans to repossess South Georgia involved landing special forces on the island to gather information about the defences. The first attempted landing was made by the SAS, who planned to disembark some distance from Leith and cross the mountains on foot, despite warnings based on local knowledge that the weather could be treacherous and that the extensively crevassed glaciers would make progress extremely difficult. On 21 April a group of SAS men were taken by helicopter to the Fortuna glacier. Conditions were poor, with high winds blasting down from the mountains. The men dug holes in the snow to protect themselves from the freezing conditions. In the morning, they realised that their position was untenable, and indeed there was a danger that some of the men would suffer seriously from exposure.

Three helicopters were sent to bring the men back. They landed in atrocious conditions and the men scrambled aboard. As the helicopters began their flight down the glacier one of them was caught in a snow squall, lost its bearings and crashed. The men, none of whom were seriously injured, were able to scramble into the other helicopters. The conditions were so bad, however, that a second helicopter crashed on to the glacier. The third helicopter returned to the ship safely. It was then able to fly back to the glacier to pick up the remaining men. Because of the appalling weather conditions and the risk that they would deteriorate further the pilot, Lieutenant-Commander Ian Stanley, decided to disregard the normal capacity of his machine and crammed all sixteen men into the helicopter, which normally should only have carried about six. He succeeded in returning to the ship and landed his machine heavily on the deck.

In London Thatcher had been informed by the Chief of Defence Staff, Admiral Lewin, of the fate of the men on the glacier and the crashed helicopters. There was a very real risk that the first action to repossess territory seized by Argentina might end in disaster. She was very relieved when news came in that the men had been safely brought back to their ship.

During the night of 22 to 23 April a landing was also attempted using inflatable dinghies, but these suffered from the strong winds and were quickly dispersed. Three of the five boats were able to land. The others were recovered later. The pace of events quickened when military intelligence in England reported that an Argentine submarine, the *Santa Fe*, was in the area. Captain Nicholas Barker of HMS *Endurance* contacted the Chief of Staff in the UK, Admiral Sir David Halifax, to discuss this: he had just received the translation of messages sent by an Argentine reconnaissance Boeing 707 that had spotted *Endurance* and given the ship's position to the submarine. The nature and clarity of the signal seemed to indicate that the submarine was only a short distance away. That night Barker was further dismayed to learn from deciphered signals that it had orders to sink his ship.

On the morning of 25 April the *Santa Fe* was spotted north of Grytviken, on the surface. Attacked by helicopters from the anti-submarine warfare ship HMS *Brilliant*, which had joined the group, and from HMS *Plymouth* and HMS *Endurance*, the submarine was damaged and beached on the shore at Leith. Any possibility of surprise was rapidly disappearing and the British forces decided to mount an invasion as quickly as possible, backed by bombardment by HMS *Antrim* and HMS *Plymouth*. The ships sent shells gradually creeping closer to the Argentine forces, and at the same time troops were flown in by helicopter near Grytviken. The garrison quickly surrendered. The Argentine forces at Leith were also persuaded to surrender, after HMS *Plymouth* threatened to bombard their positions. Alfredo Astiz, the leader of Argentine forces on the island, invited Barker to land on the football pitch to accept the surrender, but Barker changed his mind at the last minute. He later found out that the football pitch had been booby-trapped. Astiz, who was wanted by France and Sweden in connection with alleged atrocities committed during the 'dirty war', was later taken to England but, under the terms of the Geneva Convention, was eventually returned to Buenos Aires.

In London Thatcher and Nott went into Downing Street to give the news to the waiting television crews. Nott read the stiffly worded signal announcing that the White Ensign now flew alongside the Union Jack on South Georgia. The journalists immediately questioned Thatcher as to the task force's next moves; she simply invited them to 'rejoice at that news'. With the journalists continuing to press her, she walked with Nott back to the door of No. 10, and as she stepped in she told them, 'just rejoice!'. She was no doubt hugely relieved, although of course the journalists and the public could not appreciate just how pleased she was, as nobody yet knew how difficult the operation had been.

Many of the Argentine prisoners from South Georgia were taken to HMS *Endurance*. Apart from the scrap-metal workers, Astiz and some of the Argentine garrison, the prisoners also included the crew of the damaged Argentine submarine, *Santa Fe*. One of *Endurance*'s helicopter pilots knew the submarine's captain, Lieutenant-Commander Bicain, and found out that he had in fact had HMS *Endurance* in his periscope. Bicain said that he did not know exactly why he had not attempted to sink the British ship, but suggested it was because of their friendly personal relations.

As the damaged submarine was being moved away from the harbour, where it represented a hazard, an Argentine sailor was shot dead by British Marines. The Marines had been given instructions to watch the crew carefully to make sure they did not try to scuttle the submarine. Apparently the unfortunate sailor had attempted to correct a sudden change in the submarine's position, but his action had been misunderstood.

In an almost characteristic example of misread signals the significance of the re-occupation of South Georgia seems to have been interpreted quite differently in London and Buenos Aires. Britain thought it would show Argentina and the world that it meant business, and that if no negotiated settlement could be reached then Britain was prepared to use the task force. In Buenos Aires the junta seems to have thought that the action might be enough to satisfy Britain's honour, and that after this almost symbolical victory, Britain might be prepared to make more substantial concessions in the negotiations.

ARGENTINE REFUSAL OF THE HAIG PROPOSALS

After the Argentine rejection of the peace proposals on 19 April, Haig was at first inclined to abandon the attempt to achieve a negotiated settlement with the United States acting as 'honest broker', but Pym arrived in Washington on 23 April and told him Thatcher was prepared to try again. Haig prepared a fresh set of proposals. Thatcher had reservations, but asked that the proposals be put to the Argentines first. Haig asked for a meeting with the junta, but was told they did not want to see him; there had been increasing speculation about United States assistance to Britain and anti-US – and anti-Haig – feeling was running high in Buenos Aires. Haig instructed the United States Ambassador to deliver the proposals, asking the Government to reply to them by midnight on 27 April. The Argentine response, delivered after the ultimatum had expired, was negative. They wanted sovereignty, and would accept nothing less. On 30 April the United States officially announced that they would henceforth back Britain and provide military equipment and other assistance.

Meanwhile, in the South Atlantic the task force had made its first contact with the Argentine forces in the form of an Argentine Boeing 707 spy plane. For several nights the plane was intercepted by Sea Harriers but not attacked. On each occasion it turned back for home. Admiral Woodward, the task force commander, was becoming increasingly worried that the position of the task force was being monitored in this way. The Rules of Engagement were changed on 22 April to allow the British forces to attack the Boeing. On 23 April the British Government warned Argentina that any ship or aircraft threatening the task force would 'encounter the appropriate response' and concluded that 'all Argentine aircraft, including civil aircraft engaged in surveillance of [the] British forces, [would] be regarded as hostile and [were] liable to be dealt with accordingly'. That same day the characteristic radar signal of a Boeing 707 was received on HMS *Invincible*, and the carrier's Sea Dart missile system was locked on to it. A minute or so before the missile would have been launched Woodward asked his staff to plot the jet's course. Durban to Rio de Janeiro, came the reply. Woodward swiftly ordered the missile systems to be de-activated and sent a Harrier to investigate. The plane was not the Argentine intelligence Boeing, but a Brazilian airliner that had neglected to signal its position and had not responded to radio calls to identify itself. As Woodward remarks wryly in his autobiography, if he had shot the plane down there would have been such an international outcry that the task force would in all probability have simply had to turn around and go home, 'the Falklands would be the Malvinas, and [he] would have been court-martialled'. On 30 April Britain declared a total exclusion zone around the islands.

THE FIRST ATTACK, THE PERUVIAN PEACE PLAN AND UN NEGOTIATIONS

As the task force came ever closer to the Falklands, the Argentine Navy put to sea to meet it. Woodward learnt that the Argentine aircraft carrier *Veintecinco de Mayo* was to his north-west with two Exocet-armed destroyers. Further to the north was a group of three modern corvettes, each with Exocet missiles. To his south-west was the cruiser *General Belgrano* escorted by two destroyers, again armed with Exocets. One of the submarines, HMS *Spartan*, was probably close to the aircraft carrier, but had not located it and could not continue the chase as that would have meant moving into another submarine's designated patrol area (submarines are allotted clearly defined operational zones to reduce the risk of attacking another friendly submarine). HMS *Splendid*, the submarine responsible for the area into which the *Veintecinco de Mayo* had just moved, was too far away. To Woodward's intense frustration, the aircraft carrier remained undetected. Meanwhile, to the south the group led by the *Belgrano* was being shadowed by the submarine *Conqueror*. Because the activity of the first few days of May 1982 was later to become controversial, and also in order to illustrate how complex events could be during the conflict, the actions of those early days of the British campaign to repossess the Falklands will be looked at in some detail. For reasons of space, this will not, of course, be possible for all the events of the campaign.

The action began on 1 May with a long-distance bombing raid on Port Stanley airfield carried out by an RAF Vulcan bomber from Ascension. The mission was technically highly sophisticated, with no less than five air-to-air refuelling operations on the way out. A little before 4.30 a.m. local time the bomber dropped a line of heavy bombs at an angle to the runway, the first striking the runway itself, the others causing some further damage around the airfield.

Later that morning twelve Sea Harrier jump jets took off from HMS *Hermes*, which, with eleven other warships, was about 140 miles east of the Falklands, steaming towards Port Stanley. They split into three groups. The first wave of four planes reached the airfield at Port Stanley shortly after sunrise and while still out of range of anti-aircraft guns and missiles 'tossed' air-burst bombs, which explode in mid-air and send fragments over a wide area, and delayed-action bombs to disrupt the anti-aircraft defences. The second wave of five aircraft dropped parachute-retarded and cluster bombs on the airfield. The third wave attacked Goose Green airfield and a cluster bomb struck an Argentine Pucara plane which was at that very moment preparing to take off, killing the pilot and six ground crew. All the aircraft returned; one had a shell-hole in its tail. Brian Hanrahan, reporting for the BBC, was famously able to announce on BBC Radio that he had 'counted them all out' and he had 'counted them all back'.

During this time three ships, *Glamorgan*, *Arrow* and *Alacrity* had left the main carrier group to shell Stanley airfield, and were expected to arrive in the early afternoon. Two frigates, *Brilliant* and *Yarmouth*, were sent to hunt a submarine to the north of Port Stanley with their helicopters. This is believed to have been the *San Luis* which claims to have made an unsuccessful attempt to torpedo an unidentified British warship. Just after these ships had left, a pair of Argentine Mirages were detected approaching the main task force. They attacked two Sea Harriers that were flying high over Port Stanley and fired missiles at them: the Harriers were able to avoid them. Later in the afternoon three propeller-driven 'Mentor' planes took off from Pebble Island to investigate reported landings in East Falklands, but were approached by Harriers and withdrew, dropping their rockets into the sea. They were able to retreat into the cover of cloud. The Harriers themselves were later attacked by two more Mirages, which once again missed them with their missiles.

At about 4.30 p.m. local time a full-scale air offensive was launched, involving well over twenty aircraft. One Mirage was destroyed in the air, a second was damaged and later shot down by Argentine defences around Stanley as it tried to make an emergency landing. Another group of planes (Israeli-built Daggers) attacked the three ships on bombardment duty, firing at both *Arrow* and *Glamorgan*, wounding one of *Arrow*'s crew, and dropping bombs which missed *Alacrity* and *Glamorgan*, although they fell very close. Two further Daggers had been covering the attack and were approached by a pair of Sea Harriers from *Hermes* on Combat Air Patrol. One of the Daggers, flown by Jose Ardiles, the well-known football player's cousin, was hit by a Sidewinder missile. The pilot was killed. Later a Canberra bomber was shot down by another Sidewinder. The task force was also able to 'insert' special forces on to the islands to begin the essential task of collecting information on the Argentine defences.

Early the next day the *Veintecinco de Mayo* approached, intending to launch a bomb attack with Skyhawk jets to destroy the British carriers. The heavily laden Skyhawks needed a head wind to take off with a full load of fuel as well as their bombs, but, unusually, there was very little wind at all, and so the attack had to be cancelled. The British Battle Group began to move in towards the Falklands again shortly after midday local time, and this move was detected and reported to the Argentine base. An Exocet strike by a pair of Super Etendards was ordered, but had to be aborted when the refuelling operations failed.

Further to the south, the *General Belgrano* was still being followed by HMS *Conqueror*. Woodward asked for the submarines' Rules of Engagement to be modified to allow Conqueror to attack the *General Belgrano*. The War Cabinet agreed to the changes, which were signalled to the submarine at 10.30 a.m. local time (1330 GMT). The Captain did not receive the signal clearly until 14.30 p.m. local time (1730 GMT) and at 15.57 p.m. (1857 GMT) HMS *Conqueror* fired three torpedoes, two of which struck the *Belgrano*. Fire spread rapidly through the ship, and it sank less than an hour later. Over 300 Argentine sailors died.

Meanwhile, the British forces continued to look for the *Veintecinco de Mayo*, but without success. Two Argentine ships that fired on a British Sea King helicopter on anti-submarine duty were engaged by Lynx helicopters using Sea Skua anti-ship missiles. One, a patrol boat, was sunk, the other seriously damaged. On 3 May all remaining Argentine Navy vessels were ordered to steam westwards and remain in shallow water out of reach of the nuclear-powered submarines. It turned out that the Argentine Navy's warships had to all intents and purposes withdrawn from the war.

During this time President Belaunde Terry of Peru had decided to attempt further negotiation on the basis of the Haig proposals. He hoped that proposals brokered by another Latin American country would be more successful than those mediated by the United States. Indeed, he believed on 2 May that he had succeeded, and even informed the world's media that peace was assured. There is, however, little evidence that the proposals put forward by President Belaunde were acceptable to the Argentine junta. Nor is there any conclusive evidence that the British War Cabinet knew about them in any detail before the *General Belgrano* was attacked. Belaunde seems to have been under the impression that Haig had been discussing the proposals constantly with the British, but this was not the case. Pym had been told, and had responded in very general terms to what he saw as a broad framework for a fresh diplomatic move, but he did not see it as either very new or particularly promising. There is also some doubt as to whether Britain would have found the proposals any better than those put forward during General Haig's 'shuttle diplomacy'.

The attack on the *General Belgrano* seems to have hardened Argentine attitudes, and the proposals never got anywhere. The timing of the discussions and of the sinking of the *Belgrano* were later to give rise to allegations that the British War Cabinet had deliberately ordered the attack on the Argentine cruiser to 'torpedo' peace talks that it did not want (see Epilogue).

SHEFFIELD AND EXOCET

Although the threat posed by the Argentine Navy had been neutralised, the danger from the air was still very real. On 4 May the air base at Rio Grande in southern Argentina ordered a new Exocet attack by a pair of Super Etendards. This time they were successful, and a missile struck the destroyer HMS *Sheffield*. The second missile probably fell into the sea after having passed close to HMS *Yarmouth*. The warhead of the missile that hit *Sheffield* apparently did not explode, but the damage was nonetheless substantial. Twenty men were killed. This attack suddenly drove home the realisation that there would be British losses, and that Argentina was capable of launching a highly sophisticated missile attack. Although attempts were made to save it, HMS *Sheffield* sank a few days later in bad weather. Also on 4 May a Sea Harrier was shot down and its pilot killed when a second raid was launched against Goose Green. There was more bad news for the task force when two Sea Harriers were lost on 6 May. It seems likely that in very thick fog the two planes had collided. Both pilots were killed.

In Britain the prospect of further losses from Exocet attacks led to a plan being developed to destroy Argentine Super Etendards at Rio Grande. During the evening of 17 May HMS *Invincible* steamed fast towards the mainland to allow a helicopter to fly an SAS team in complete darkness to a location somewhere close to the base in Patagonia. The helicopter, which did not have enough fuel to return to the task force, then flew on to Chile and was burnt. The crew later gave themselves up to the Chilean authorities and claimed they had got lost and been forced to make an emergency landing. Meanwhile, according to one account, the SAS team found that a mistake had been made and they had landed some

50 miles from the pre-arranged spot. They were therefore too far from the airfield to pursue the attack, and escaped over land to Chile. As any hope of surprise had been lost with the announcement of the discovery of the burnt-out helicopter the plans were dropped. Further ideas to attack the airfield by making a surprise landing from a Hercules transport plane were considered, but then abandoned after the SAS expressed their disquiet concerning what they felt were the very slight chances of success for such a daring frontal assault.

DIPLOMATIC ULTIMATUM

After the failure of the Haig initiative, further diplomatic moves were made by Javier Perez de Cuellar, the UN Secretary-General. In the wake of the *Belgrano* action, Britain was coming under increasing pressure to reach a negotiated settlement. Thatcher no longer believed – if she had ever believed it – that the Argentines were negotiating in good faith. She thought they were simply playing for time, and with the onset of winter only weeks away, time was something the task force most definitely did not have.

It was nonetheless decided that an attempt should be made. Britain had to be seen to be negotiating in good faith to maintain international support. On

Sunday 16 May, at a meeting at Chequers, Thatcher asked Sir Nicholas Henderson, Ambassador to Washington, and Sir Anthony Parsons to report on the situation in the USA and in the UN, and help draft a final offer which the Argentine government would have two days to accept or reject. The War Cabinet, civil servants and diplomats worked out a proposal that would have given Argentina a lot more than Thatcher doubtless felt happy about.

The proposed agreement specified that it was without prejudice to any sovereignty rights or claims of either party. It provided a detailed timetable for the withdrawal of both parties and the lifting of exclusion zones and sanctions. The islands would be placed under a UN administrator agreeable to both parties who would work in consultation with the representative institutions already operating on the islands (in accordance with article 73 of the United Nations charter), along with an Argentine representative. The Communications Agreement of the early 1970s would be reactivated, and a joint consultative committee set up. Negotiations would then be started with the aim of achieving a solution by 31 December 1982, without prejudice to the outcome.

Parsons took the offer personally to New York and showed it to Perez de Cuellar. He was astonished at just how much the British Government was prepared to give. There is every likelihood that, had it been accepted, the British Government would have been placed in the greatest difficulty by Parliament. As it happened, the junta rejected the proposals. Parsons recalls commenting sadly to the Secretary-General that because of this many young men would have to die before a solution was reached.

LANDING AT SAN CARLOS

After much discussion it was finally decided that the British landings should take place on the west coast of East Falkland, in San Carlos Water. The choice represented a compromise between the Navy's need for a relatively safe place for the landing ships and the ground force's desire to be as close as possible to the final objective. The hills around San Carlos Water provided some protection against air attack, although, as the task force was to learn very soon, they did not rule it out entirely. Special forces on the islands had been able to establish that the area was only lightly defended.

On the night of 14/15 May, in preparation for the landing, an airstrip on Pebble Island, to the north of West Falkland and quite close to the entrance to

Falkland Sound, was attacked by SAS forces backed up by naval shelling. A number of Argentine Pucara counter-insurgency planes were destroyed on the ground. The British troops suffered only very light casualties.

The landings, code-named Operation Sutton, took place on the night of 21 May. There were very few casualties (the crews of two light helicopters) and this has meant that the risks taken have tended to be forgotten. And yet, for almost two hours practically defenceless landing craft made their way down to San Carlos Water to their landing beaches. Had the Argentine defenders been more vigilant they could have posed a serious threat to the landing forces.

The response from Argentine aircraft was not long in coming. A sustained air offensive took place throughout the rest of the day, before the Rapier anti-aircraft missile systems could become fully effective. The frigate HMS *Ardent* was caught by Argentine planes as she steamed north up Falkland Sound after shelling Goose Green. It tried to limp to the shelter of San Carlos Water but was caught by a new wave of planes. Hit by several bombs, she finally sank during the night, with the loss of twenty-two men.

The Argentine pilots impressed everyone who saw them with their skill and courage. Some were shot down by Combat Air Patrols, others were destroyed by guns and missiles. The British sailors called the area 'Bomb Alley', the Argentine pilots the 'Valley of Death'.

The pilots attacked the warships, not the supply ships, which was probably a severe tactical error. All day the huge silhouette of *Canberra* stood in San Carlos Water. The white-painted liner, known by the sailors as the 'Great White Whale', was such a huge target that it seemed incomprehensible that she had not been attacked. It appears that some of the pilots assumed she was a hospital ship and she was therefore largely left alone. It is also likely that as they flew in fast and low the pilots had very little time to select a target and so chose the first ship they could get a clear run at. These would naturally be the picket missile ships rather than the supply ships or troop carriers. Apart from *Ardent*, HMS *Argonaut* and HMS *Antrim* were both struck by bombs which failed to explode, and HMS *Broadsword* and HMS *Brilliant* were strafed.

It has been said that the task force was extremely lucky that so many bombs failed to go off, and sometimes argued that this was the fault of poor preparation by the Argentines. It is true that if all the bombs that hit British ships had gone off the damage and loss of life would have been much greater. Against that it has been pointed out that the reason why so many bombs failed to explode was that the planes were forced by British missiles and guns to fly in at very low levels to avoid being shot down as they approached, so low that the bombs did not have time to fuse before they struck their targets.

During the following days there was more air activity. HMS *Antelope* was hit by two bombs on 23 May, one of which exploded as a bomb-disposal expert tried to defuse it, and *Antelope* was fatally damaged in the huge explosion which was captured in a memorable photograph. An Argentine Exocet attack launched that afternoon was aborted after the planes failed to locate their targets. On 24 May the landing ships *Sir Galahad* and *Sir Lancelot* were both hit by bombs which did not explode and *Sir Bedivere* by a bomb which damaged the ship and then exploded in water.

On 25 May, Argentina's national day, there were more major Argentine air attacks. Woodward had placed a two ship 'missile trap' north-west of the entrance to Falkland Sound. This was made up of a destroyer, HMS *Coventry*, a sister ship to HMS *Sheffield*, and a frigate, HMS *Broadsword*, both armed with effective missile systems. In the early afternoon after a number of other raids Argentine aircraft were detected approaching the ships. Two Sea Harriers flew towards the area, but were told to stay away lest they should get in the way of the ships' missiles. As the Argentine planes approached, HMS *Coventry*'s missile system failed to lock on to the target, and she manoeuvred fast to evade the attack. HMS *Brilliant* trained its Sea Dart system on the incoming planes, but just as they came into range, HMS *Coventry* swerved across in front of her and the missile launch had to be aborted. *Coventry* was hit by three bombs, properly fused and properly delivered, and sank only a few minutes later; Argentine air losses during these attacks were heavy.

Another major blow came when two Super Etendards carried out another Exocet attack on the carrier group. The carriers and their escorts fired 'chaff', millions of little pieces of plastic coated with aluminium, to act as a decoy and lure the missiles away from the ships themselves. The merchant ship *Atlantic Conveyor* had no such protection and was struck by one of the two Exocets. There is some doubt as to what happened to the other missile: it may have been deflected away from the ships and have fallen harmlessly into the sea. *Atlantic Conveyor* was seriously damaged as fire raged through her, destroying much-needed supplies, including several helicopters, especially troop-carrying Chinooks, tents for the troops on the Falklands and metal matting with which it had been intended to build a temporary landing and take-off strip on the islands for the Harriers. The ship was completely burnt out and later sank; twelve men were killed, including the ship's captain.

GOOSE GREEN

Brigadier Julian Thompson, in charge of the troops on shore until the arrival of Major-General Jeremy Moore, who was at the time travelling down to the South Atlantic on the *QE2*, had orders to establish a secure beachhead, but not to begin advancing against Argentine positions. He was, however, making plans for a break-out, relying heavily on the use of troop-carrying helicopters.

In London there was mounting pressure for something to happen. There was a fear that the British forces might get bogged down and take a long time to break out from the beachhead, just as the Allied forces in Normandy had been stuck for a long time before they could move forwards. It was also felt that Britain's diplomatic position might be weakened if no moves were made soon. Cecil Parkinson, the leader of the Conservative Party and a member of the War Cabinet, said, 'Having established a secure base we are planning to move and to move fast. It is not our intention to be lured into a long and bloody war'.

On 25 May Brigadier Thompson sent an SAS unit to reconnoitre Mount Kent. He also ordered Lieutenant-Colonel 'H' Jones of the 2nd battalion, the Parachute Regiment (2 Para) to carry out a raid on Goose Green. One of Jones' companies advanced to a position a little to the north of Darwin and Goose Green, but the raid had to be cancelled when bad weather closed in and prevented helicopters from bringing in the guns that were to provide artillery support. Jones, who was apparently intensely annoyed, was ordered to move back to his positions on Sussex Mountain. That evening Thompson learnt of the loss of Chinook helicopters on the *Atlantic Conveyor*, leaving only one for duty on the Falklands. He had to scrap the plans he had been working on and start again. With so few helicopters there would be no alternative for most of the troops but to travel the 60 miles or more from San Carlos to Port Stanley on foot, carrying as much ammunition and supplies as possible.

The following day Thompson was ordered to launch an attack on Goose Green. He would have preferred to give priority to securing Mount Kent, but was given explicit orders from the headquarters of the Commander-in-Chief of the Fleet at Northwood, near London. 'H' Jones set off with 2 Para as night was falling on the evening of 26 May to Camilla Creek House, a short distance to the

north of the battle zone. The next morning Goose
Green was attacked by Harriers; one plane was shot
down. Patrols were sent out to acquire information
on the enemy positions. At about midday Jones was
told that the BBC World Service had just reported
that 2 Para were advancing on Darwin. Furious,
Jones ordered his men to take cover against the
attack that would surely follow, but none came. It
would appear that the Argentine commanding
officer took no notice of the BBC broadcast,
believing that it was a psychological operation.
Goose Green was reinforced by troops taken from
Mount Kent, but not, apparently, because of any
premature announcements on the BBC or
elsewhere.

The attack began in the early hours of 28 May. It
soon ran behind schedule. Gunfire support from
HMS *Arrow* had to be stopped for a few hours during
the night because of a fault but the advance went
well. As day broke, however, 2 Para found themselves
having to move across open country under heavy
fire. HMS *Arrow* had withdrawn and the Harriers
could not provide support because of fog at sea. At
one point Jones went forward to see why the advance
had apparently run out of momentum. He decided
to take action himself and charged an Argentine
position. He was hit and mortally wounded by fire

from another Argentine position that he had not seen. For this act of bravery Jones was awarded the Victoria Cross. A helicopter that had been ordered in to evacuate the wounded was attacked by Pucara planes and shot down.

Command was taken over by Major Keeble. The fighting continued throughout 28 May. At one stage there was confusion as British soldiers went as they believed to negotiate an Argentine surrender, having apparently seen white flags being waved from one of the Argentine positions. It would seem that as a result of misunderstandings the men were shot at and killed. There are differing accounts of the incident, and it will perhaps never be known exactly what happened. As the troops got closer to Goose Green they were attacked by Skyhawks and Pucaras; one of the Pucaras was shot down by a Blowpipe missile. In the afternoon Harriers were finally able to launch an attack on Argentine positions at Goose Green, and by nightfall 2 Para had surrounded the settlement. Keeble sent prisoners with a message inviting the Argentine forces to surrender; if they did not they would be bombarded. During the night 2 Para were reinforced, and the threatened bombardment was prepared. But it was not necessary – in the morning the Argentine garrison did surrender.

Major Keeble and his men were astonished at the number of prisoners. Many of them were in fact non-combatant support personnel working on the aircraft that flew from the airfield. The battle may not have been necessary from a purely strategic point of view, but it did provide the military success that the politicians had wanted and gave the British attacking forces a psychological advantage. It was considered normal for an attacking force to be at least three times as strong as the defenders, but 2 Para had enjoyed no such numerical superiority. In total eighteen British servicemen died and over fifty Argentines.

Shortly after the battle for Goose Green Pope John-Paul II arrived for a visit to Britain. He had thought hard about whether he should come at all, and only in the end agreed to do so on the understanding that he would not meet politicians, and would go on to visit Buenos Aires afterwards. John-Paul II told the faithful assembled at Coventry Cathedral on 30 May that: 'Today, the scale and horror of international warfare – whether nuclear or not – makes it totally unacceptable as a means of settling differences between nations. War should belong to the tragic past, to history. It should find no place on humanity's agenda for the future.'

While 'H' Jones and 2 Para had been preparing to launch their attack on Goose Green, 45 Commando had set off on its 'yomp', and 3 Para had begun its 'tab' towards Douglas and Teal Inlet along the northern routes, both carrying extremely heavy loads ('yomp' and 'tab' were services slang for the same thing: a march). On 30 May Douglas and Teal Settlement were in British hands. 42 Commando were able to secure Mount Kent and Mount Challenger, key high points on the way to Stanley. The early days of June were marked by various skirmishes and minor engagements.

Argentina launched its last air-borne Exocet on 30 May in a combined attack involving two Super Etendards and a number of Skyhawks. The missile was launched normally but did not hit anything. The Argentine Skyhawk pilots who followed the Super Etendards incorrectly reported that HMS *Invincible* had been hit. Two of the Skyhawks were shot down before they reached their target – not *Invincible* but HMS *Avenger* – while the other two dropped their bombs, which missed, and returned to base.

UN CALLS FOR A CEASE-FIRE

The fighting had not put an end to the diplomatic moves. Reagan telephoned Thatcher on 31 May and pleaded with her not to inflict too serious a defeat on the Argentines. She responded 'forcefully' that

Britain had not lost ships and lives merely to hand the islands over to a third party. The United Nations Security Council met on 4 June to discuss a resolution put forward by Spain and Panama, calling for an immediate cease-fire. Britain vetoed the resolution. Despite Jeane Kirkpatrick's own reservations, she followed the instructions she had been given and also vetoed the resolution. A short while after the vote she was told that the instructions had changed and that she was to abstain. It was too late, but she informed the Security Council that had she been able to change her vote she would have done so. The impression of confusion generated by this incident drew media attention away from Britain's use of the veto which might otherwise have attracted more critical comment. From that point on attempts to achieve a negotiated solution were pursued less energetically, as the military option had clearly taken over.

5 BRIGADE AND DISASTER AT FITZROY

In the Falklands the advance along the southern route was entrusted to 5 Brigade, which had just arrived in San Carlos (on 1 June). It had been rapidly assembled and sent to join 3 Brigade when the commanders realised just how strong the

Argentine defences were. 2 Para now joined
5 Brigade, which also included Gurkhas and Welsh
and Scots Guards. 2 Para was keen to move on, and
used a phone line that had remained intact to
establish that Bluff Cove and Fitzroy were not
defended by Argentine forces. A group of about
eighty soldiers commandeered a Chinook helicopter
which fortuitously passed their way and moved
quickly forward to take the undefended settlement.
A few more men managed to find helicopters to join
them. They had to be reinforced rapidly, however,
and with the chronic shortage of helicopters there
was only one way for the main body of troops from 5
Brigade to make rapid progress to join them, and
that was by sea. Because there were fears that
Argentine forces in Port Stanley now had a land-
based Exocet it would be dangerous for the assault
ships to take the troops into Bluff Cove and Fitzroy
and the final leg of the journey would have to be
done in smaller craft.

On the night of 5 June the Scots Guards were
taken to a point off the south coast of East Falkland
by the assault ship *Intrepid* and then on to Bluff Cove
by landing craft – a long, unpleasant and dangerous
journey. The following night *Fearless* took the Welsh
Guards to the same rendezvous point, but the
landing craft that were to have met her to ferry the

men to Bluff Cove were unable to make the journey, and only half of the men were able to continue in *Fearless'* own two landing craft. The rest were taken back to San Carlos. On the night of 7 June the Royal Fleet Auxiliary *Sir Galahad* left San Carlos with the remaining Welsh guardsmen, and joined *Sir Tristram* in Port Pleasant, to the south of Fitzroy, early the following morning. Faced with the prospect of a march to Bluff Cove and the risk of being separated from their heavy equipment, the guardsmen's officers were at first reluctant to disembark at Fitzroy, despite being strongly advised to do so. When finally a solution was found to take them to Bluff Cove, a technical hitch further delayed the process.

The ships had been seen by Argentine spotters up in the hills, who called an air strike. On 8 June two groups of Argentine planes were ordered to attack. A group of Daggers spotted HMS *Plymouth* in Falkland Sound before they reached the Fitzroy area and attacked it. Four bombs hit the ship, but none of them exploded. *Plymouth* survived. Further east, a group of Skyhawks bombed *Sir Tristram* and *Sir Galahad,* causing substantial loss of life and damage. Helicopter pilots bravely flew in to rescue survivors, despite the fire and explosions. In total fifty men were killed, and many more were horribly burnt or wounded. In Choiseul Sound a group of

Skyhawks bombed and destroyed a landing craft, killing six men. Three of the Skyhawks were shot down by Sea Harriers.

BATTLES FOR THE HIGH GROUND

The main advance towards Stanley continued in two phases. In the first phase, which began on the night of 11 June, attacks were mounted against well-prepared defensive positions on Mount Longdon, Two Sisters and Mount Harriet. The fighting was heavy, especially on Mount Longdon, and twenty-two British soldiers were killed. During the fighting Sergeant Ian McKay of 3 Para was killed bravely attacking Argentine positions. He was awarded the second Victoria Cross of the campaign. Out at sea HMS *Glamorgan*, which had been bombarding positions around Port Stanley, was hit by a land-based Exocet as it withdrew from its position on the morning of 12 June, and thirteen men were killed. During the night of 11 to 12 June a British shell struck a house in Stanley and killed three women, the only Falklanders to lose their lives during the assault. Two days later, in the second phase of fighting for the high ground over Stanley, Wireless Ridge, Tumbledown Mountain and Mount William were all taken. Again, there was strong resistance, especially on Tumbledown Mountain, and twenty men were killed.

WHITE FLAGS

The Argentine resistance began to crumble, and soldiers were seen moving back into Stanley. A cease-fire was ordered and negotiations began with General Menéndez and the instrument of surrender was finally signed during the evening of 14 June in the presence of Major General Moore. There are no photographs of the signing, as Moore was keen to avoid any risk that the presence of war correspondents might delay the end of the fighting. It had been, he said, borrowing Wellington's phrase, a 'damned close-run thing': some of his gunners were almost out of ammunition.

It was a remarkable achievement by any standard. The servicemen had little opportunity to relax, however. The surrender covered only the Falklands themselves, and so attack was still possible from the mainland. There was also the urgent need to deal with several thousand prisoners, who would suffer from exposure if they were not given shelter. The tents that might have protected them from the elements had been destroyed on *Atlantic Conveyor*. The campaign did not quite come to an end with the surrender at Port Stanley. There remained the base at Southern Thule, which had been set up in 1976. On 20 June groups of Marines were flown on to the island in HMS *Endurance*'s helicopter, and the accompanying warships prepared to give a demonstration of their firepower. Minutes before the bombardment was due to begin the Argentines surrendered.

FIVE

Information Management and Misperceptions

INFORMATION MANAGEMENT

In the early 1980s when the Falklands crisis broke out the media had begun to believe that the development of electronic news-gathering equipment, linked to the possibility of satellite transmission of television pictures, would mean more immediate coverage of major events. News would be brought to the public as it happened. The disappointment that developed about the conditions in which the war correspondents worked may need to be set against these expectations.

The Falklands War gave little opportunity for the use of this new technology. The Government claimed that it was not possible to use satellites to transmit television pictures, for to do so would require diverting almost the entire transmission capacity available in the South Atlantic for this purpose, an option that was militarily unacceptable. It did gradually become easier to send still pictures, as technical solutions were found to solve some of the problems of getting news from the South Atlantic to Britain, although newspaper editors were suspicious when this technology was first used to transmit a picture of British troops being welcomed by islanders. The Government claimed that it thought editors would be keen to use this picture; cynics suggested that the propaganda value of the photograph was also a factor in the speed with which it was sent.

As a result of the technical constraints on sending back television pictures, combined with the speed with which the land war developed, no television footage of fighting on the islands was shown in Britain until the war was practically over. There is no evidence that the technical arguments put forward by the Government were not perfectly valid. There is little doubt that the Government was much happier that this was so. There had been fear of a 'Vietnam syndrome': coverage of the horrors of war might weaken the resolve and lower the morale of the British public, which could be detrimental to the war effort just as the daily diet of news from Vietnam had sapped the American will to fight, according to the interpretation still favoured in US military circles. The result in the Falklands was a conflict in which very few images of injury and death were shown to the public before it was all over.

The information that was given, however, both by spokesmen in London and by the war correspondents who embarked with the task force, was on the whole accurate and not unreasonably delayed. The difficulties that journalists had to face were, it is true, considerable. Right from the start they had problems even getting authorisation to sail with the task force. The Navy originally showed little enthusiasm for taking any war correspondents at all. Pressure was brought to bear, however, and a small number of journalists were accredited to join the ships bound for the South Atlantic, although no foreign journalists were allowed to sail. The often disorganised and precipitate circumstances of the departure of those correspondents who were authorised to join the task force meant that some were not well prepared for the campaign. Procedures for vetting, clearing or censoring copy were naturally controversial. Access to the action was not always easy, and not always authorised. Journalists were very much aggrieved and frustrated when their copy was delayed, for whatever reason, especially if that delay meant that they would miss deadlines in London. This could well mean that the information would be announced officially in London before the war correspondents' copy became available. Like all 'stale' news, their reports would then be relegated to the inside pages. Tempers were sometimes frayed as war correspondents, working in difficult circumstances, exposed to the very real dangers of the war and the rigours of the climate, found themselves 'scooped' by the Ministry of Defence's spokesman in London, Ian MacDonald.

In London, speaking in the House of Commons on the day after the loss of HMS *Sheffield* was announced, Thatcher expressed concern that radio and television were not putting the British case 'fully and effectively'. She was offended by the way some commentators treated British and Argentines 'almost on a neutral basis', and would clearly have preferred them to talk in terms of 'our forces' and 'the enemy'. A few days later this dissatisfaction boiled over after the BBC *Panorama* programme presented views of the conflict from both sides. The Conservative MP Sir Bernard Braine said that for many people it was practically treachery. Others, like the Labour leader Michael Foot, thought the BBC were trying to do their duty in difficult circumstances, and indeed opinion polls later showed that public opinion supported the BBC. Foot was more worried by what he saw as the excesses of the popular press, referring to 'the hysterical bloodlust of the *Sun* and the *Daily Mail*'. It was the *Sun* that produced probably the most memorable, 'gung-ho' front page of the war, when it greeted news of the successful attack against the *General Belgrano* with the banner headline 'GOTCHA!' in large, bold capital letters, although this was changed in later editions as the scale of the loss of life became apparent. All of this was no doubt regrettable. But it did not mean that the public was grossly misinformed. There was no major revelation after the conflict of substantial information that had been hidden or withheld unduly, with the possible exception of the circumstances surrounding the sinking of the *Belgrano*.

MISPERCEPTIONS

To a large extent then the facts of the campaign were generally – but not always – made known to the public within a reasonable time, but the extremely important overall impressions of the conflict were perhaps misleading because of the delays surrounding the availability of pictures. Another thing that was not always available, despite the recourse to 'armchair generals' and other would-be specialists, was any clear idea of the 'bigger picture'. There could be no hard information about the overall plans, strategies and tactical decisions taken by the commanders, and without such information, interpretation of the meaning of events could be inaccurate. It was not always possible to make sense of events. A revealing example of this is the way in which the events of the first few days of May were misinterpreted.

As the task force progressed southwards, observers noted a gradual hardening of Britain's military response. On 12 April a maritime exclusion zone was declared. On 23 April the Government warned Argentina that any military ships or planes representing a threat to the task force would be dealt with appropriately. Two days later South Georgia was recaptured, and on 30 April Britain declared a total exclusion zone. On 1 May news came in of the Vulcan bombing attack on the airfield, followed by the Harrier attack on Stanley airfield and Goose Green, and naval bombardment of targets around Port Stanley, as well as the first engagements with Argentine aircraft. This was interpreted as a gradual increase in the imposition of force, entirely consistent with the theory of gradual escalation. Moreover, the general perception was still that the task force was primarily a weapon in a diplomatic war, strengthening Britain's negotiating position, carefully and progressively piling on the pressure.

The ideal of gradual escalation suggests that a belligerent is able to control events to a substantial extent and manage its responses carefully, so as to escalate the conflict only as much as is strictly necessary to achieve its objectives. Another concept that may be appropriate in this context is the 'just war' principle of proportionality. Within this Christian theory war can, under certain circumstances, be justified, but at all times the means employed must be proportional to the situation, rather as they should be in more mundane self-defence. Britain's actions as its task force got closer to the islands could be seen, and indeed were widely seen, as the carefully managed application of force in gradually increasing quantity in pursuit of a clearly identified objective, assumed to be the essentially diplomatic goal of Argentine withdrawal and subsequent negotiations over ultimate sovereignty.

This was not at all the perception of events that underlay the tactics adopted by the task force commander. Woodward knew that he only had limited time in which to achieve his objective, which was to enable a landing on the Falkland Islands. Any such landing would be impossibly costly if opposed by the full force of Argentina's Navy and Air Force. He sought therefore to engage Argentine ships and aircraft before attempting any amphibious operation. Argentina, however, could be expected to keep its forces in reserve until a landing was taking place, when it would be able to create maximum damage at minimum risk. British ships and aircraft would be tied up protecting the landing operations and would not be free to engage the Argentine forces. Woodward, therefore, deliberately attempted to trick the Argentine high command into thinking he was going to effect a landing immediately. He calculated that the Argentines would be inclined to believe the attack would be planned in the same way the United States forces would do it – Argentina was familiar with American tactics and might be expected to assume that Britain, one of the United States' closest allies, would act in more or less the same manner – and that is to bring its full force to bear directly on the final target. So Woodward set out to simulate a full frontal attack on Port Stanley. He was, however, worried. The task force was vulnerable. He knew that Argentina had reasonably good information as to his whereabouts; he, however, had been unable to find the aircraft carrier *Veintecinco de Mayo*, which had Skyhawks capable of carrying out bombing missions and was escorted by two modern destroyers. There were also three more frigates that he had not been able to locate, and there was still a possible threat from submarines.

So Woodward was not applying force in an orderly, measured, gradual process of escalation in support of diplomacy, he was manoeuvring into a full-scale battle.

Careful management of the amount of force applied would have required a degree of control over events that was impossible with British forces stretched to the limit almost 8,000 miles from home. On 1 May an Argentine submarine probably tried to sink a British ship. On 2 May Argentina tried to launch a bomb attack from its aircraft carrier, but was thwarted because of the lack of wind. It tried to carry out an Exocet strike from land-based Super Etendards, but the in flight refuelling failed Argentine planes bombed the ships Woodward sent to shell the area around Port Stanley and could have sunk one or more of them if the bombs had fallen just a little closer. Equally, if British submarines had been able to find the Argentine aircraft carrier there is every possibility that it would have been attacked and sunk.

Against this background the action against the *Belgrano* seems much less of a sudden escalation of the conflict. As Woodward writes in his account of the war, looking back on the events of 1 May, 'I do not believe that, back home in the UK, people had any idea how viciously this war had begun.' This basic misperception also explains how the sinking of HMS *Sheffield* was seen as a reprisal for the sinking of the *Belgrano*. The Labour MP Tam Dalyell, for example, has written: 'I believe – no *Belgrano*, no *Sheffield*, no *Ardent*, no *Antelope*, no *Atlantic Conveyor*, no *Coventry*, no Goose Green, no Bluff Cove.' Yet, as we have seen, attempts had been made to use Exocet missiles against task force ships before the attack on the *Belgrano* and before the successful attack against HMS *Sheffield*.

The inaccurate picture projected by the media in Britain of the opening engagements in the battle to repossess the Falklands was not the result of deliberate misinformation, but rather of a perfectly normal situation in which a military leader does not reveal details of his plans. The experience of the Falklands raised doubts about the ability of any news reporting to present an accurate narrative of a conflict while military operations are still going on. In brief, the Falklands war showed clearly that modern technology offers no real, novel solution to the essential paradox that the successful conduct of war requires some degree of secrecy, while successful journalism needs quite the opposite.

SIX

International Reactions and Perceptions

OFFICIAL REACTIONS

Unusually, perhaps uniquely in the post-war world, responses abroad to the crisis in the South Atlantic followed neither east–west nor north–south divisions. Even in Latin America, which had little enthusiasm for Britain's presence in the hemisphere, reactions were far from uniform. There, as indeed in many other parts of the world, a distinction was drawn between the sovereignty dispute, on the one hand, and Argentina's use of military force to occupy the islands, on the other. Argentina in fact enjoyed substantial support for its claim to sovereignty over the Malvinas, but solidarity on that particular issue did not always extend to supporting the general principle of using force to resolve sovereignty disputes. A number of Latin American countries had territorial disputes with powerful neighbours, and had no wish to fall victim themselves to some similar *coup de main*.

Most significant in this context was the position of Argentina's neighbour Chile. There had been a long-standing dispute over the sovereignty of three small islands in the extreme south of the Latin American cone, in the Beagle Channel. Attempts to resolve the dispute through international arbitration foundered against Argentine intransigence, and there was a real fear in Chile that Argentina would go to war to repossess the islands. Chile was notably restrained in its support for Argentina. The existence of tension between Chile and Argentina indirectly helped Britain because Argentina was obliged to maintain a garrison of well-trained and well-equipped troops along the Chilean frontier. Later, as Britain took action to repossess the Falklands, Chile agreed at the very least to turn a blind eye to some British actions, and gave valuable intelligence support.

Another South American country that felt uncomfortable about Argentina's use of force was Colombia. Colombia feared that its neighbour Nicaragua, which claimed sovereignty over a group of small islands, might follow the junta's example. Most Latin American countries, however, publicly supported Argentina; whatever the misgivings some of them may have had about Argentina's methods, they mostly closed ranks behind their neighbour. Venezuela, Colombia, Peru, Ecuador and Bolivia agreed to step up trade with Argentina to help it overcome the EEC boycott. Panama gave Argentina its fullest support, right from the beginning, voting against Security Council Resolution 502 on 3 April. Peru and Bolivia offered military assistance. Venezuela demanded 'hemisphere' solidarity with Argentina. Cuba and Nicaragua also supported Argentina, not out of any sense of ideological *rapprochement*, but essentially because of shared anti-colonialism. The Organisation of American States sided with Argentina, but it never went much further than verbal backing. At a meeting held on 28 April 1982 it supported Argentina's sovereignty claim but called on both parties to negotiate. The English-speaking Caribbean countries stressed the idea of self-determination for the islanders. Later in the conflict, on 29 May, the OAS condemned Britain's attack on the Falkland Islands and called on the United States to stop helping Britain. Only four countries abstained: the United States, Chile, Colombia and Trinidad and Tobago.

As the United States was the most influential country in the Americas, its position with regard to the growing crisis was crucially important. Britain remembered only too well how the lack of support from the United States led to the Suez fiasco in 1956. Argentina was convinced that the United States would not take sides, and felt that without American aid Britain would not be able to mount a successful military campaign to repossess the Falklands.

To begin with, as we have seen, the United States took an officially neutral stand, arguing that if it were to be able to help bring about a peaceful solution it had to be able to play the 'honest broker'. Unofficially, the United States gave substantial logistics support right from the very start, with the Defense Secretary Caspar Weinberger giving personal authorisation for delivery to Britain of weapons, fuel and other supplies with unprecedented speed. Britain's gratitude for Weinberger's friendship was expressed shortly after the war when he was given an honorary knighthood. There is some doubt as to how much the President knew of the scale of the support given to Britain by the Pentagon. Caspar Weinberger is said in a private conversation with Nicholas Henderson to have offered Britain the use of an aircraft carrier in the event of either the *Invincible* or *Hermes* being sunk. This unofficial aid was, however, given amid the greatest secrecy, and the official neutral stance was roundly criticised in Britain. When, at the end of April, Argentina rejected the peace proposals hammered out between

Haig and the British Government, the United States finally came down decisively behind the United Kingdom. The United States could not allow a valuable European ally to be defeated by a country that had flouted the principles of international law. Once the conflict was over, however, the United States supported the United Nations' call on Britain to negotiate with Argentina.

It might have been expected that any action supported by the United States, involving an issue that many saw as the last fling of an imperial nation, would have attracted the unqualified opposition of the Soviet Union. The Soviet Union did criticise what it referred to as Britain's colonialism. It had been progressively building closer links with Argentina, buying three-quarters of the country's grain exports in 1982 after economic sanctions were imposed by most Western countries in protest against the Soviet intervention in Afghanistan. But in the Security Council, the Soviet Union did not veto Resolution 502: it abstained, no doubt uneasy about the implications of supporting Argentina's use of force to settle a territorial dispute. It later gave political and diplomatic support to Argentina, although Argentina did not seek any material assistance from the Soviet Union in the form of military hardware.

Responses in Europe again blurred the predominant fault lines of east–west and north–south. A whole range of sometimes conflicting considerations entered into the debate. All the countries of the European Economic Community supported Britain's call for sanctions at the very beginning of the conflict, but this unity was gradually weakened, although never destroyed, by the misgivings of at least two EEC member States, Ireland and Italy. Outside the EEC, Spain also had reservations.

Among the first European heads of state to convey a message of support to Thatcher was France's President François Mitterrand, followed closely by the West German Chancellor Helmut Schmidt. Both countries were worried by the breach of international law that Argentina's aggression represented. West Germany may well have thought of West Berlin; France also had a number of small islands scattered across the globe that would be difficult to defend against a determined predatory neighbour.

Both Italy and Spain had close historical, cultural and economic ties with Argentina. There were of course a large number of Argentines of Spanish descent, but almost half the population of Argentina had some Italian blood, including Galtieri himself. There were indeed over a million Italian citizens living in Argentina. Italy's support for Britain gradually waned until it refused to extend economic sanctions when they came up for renewal in May. Spain was in some difficulty over the issue. It was keen to join the European Community, and needed Britain's support. Its position was further complicated by the fact that it also had a territorial dispute with Britain, over Gibraltar, and saw some 'linkage' there. The third major factor shaping Spain's response to the crisis was the special relationship it had with its transatlantic 'brothers' and its ambition to provide a bridge between Europe and Latin America. While its foreign policy seemed to be moving towards closer links with Europe, which might also help it resolve the problem of Gibraltar, it could not neglect its historical ties with South America. Its response to the Falklands crisis was somewhat ambiguous as a result. The Spanish Government announced shortly after the Argentine invasion that it had always supported decolonisation for the Falkland Islands and the re-establishment of Argentina's territorial integrity, and indeed it abstained on Resolution 502 because it made no mention of this aspect of the conflict. Spain also refused to join the economic sanctions imposed by the European Community, for the same reason. At the same time it consistently made it clear that it did not support the use of force, and called on both parties to work to achieve a negotiated settlement.

On 2 June, with Panama, it presented the draft resolution to the Security Council calling for an immediate cease-fire. It joined NATO at the end of May 1982, at the height of the fighting, and on 4 June expressed its disapproval of Britain's military response, thus breaking NATO's hitherto unanimous support for the United Kingdom.

Ireland's position was even more complex. There was a substantial population of Irish origin in Argentina, although nowhere near as large as the number of people with Spanish and Italian roots. But Ireland also had a tradition of neutrality which it had exercised during the Second World War in particular. Also of significance was the fact of the historical rift between Ireland and Britain, and there was still a powerful nationalist strand to Irish politics. This was exacerbated by the vulnerability of the Irish Government in 1982, with a beleaguered Taoiseach Charles Haughey hanging on to power with a tiny majority and an impending by-election in which the nationalist dimension could be decisive. After the loss of the *General Belgrano*, public opinion in Ireland hardened against Britain: the Defence Secretary even accused Britain of acting in much the same way as a 'hit and run driver', although this was no doubt also inspired by an accident a week or two earlier in which a British submarine had sunk an Irish fishing boat and failed to come to the assistance of the crew. Haughey rejected this extreme position from a minister who in any case had something of a reputation for his outspoken views, but he probably represented a significant minority opinion harbouring residual hostility to perceived British colonialism.

REACTIONS IN THE PRESS – MISPERCEPTIONS?

Although there were exceptions to the general support for the British Government's action in the British media, readers at the time could be excused for thinking that there was some sort of broad consensus regarding the significance of the conflict and the issues of principle it raised. This perception can usefully be tempered by looking, if only very briefly, at this aspect of the way the events of the South Atlantic were presented in other countries.

While the British and Argentine press were more or less diametrically opposed in their assessment of the rights and wrongs of the crisis, they did at least agree that the whole business was a deeply serious one. This view, however, was at best unevenly shared in other countries. The major United States newspapers did see the serious side, but in many other countries the press just could not understand why two advanced nations were prepared to countenance war over such remote territory. They shared the view that the conflict was like two bald men fighting over a comb.

This inability to share the sense of importance behind the issue meant that it could initially be seen as at least anachronistic, and at most somewhat farcical. But any such wryly bemused response to the prospect of the might of the Royal Navy being dispatched to deal with the 'tin-pot dictators' of the Argentine junta dissolved overnight when news of the destruction of the *General Belgrano*, with substantial loss of life, reached newsrooms on 3 May. For example, on 8 May, the *Irish Times* wrote in an editorial: 'The longer this tragic crisis continues, the more preposterous and disproportionate it looks', although it continued to consider that Argentina had been in the wrong when it occupied the islands. A few days later it criticised the self-indulgence of both Britain and Argentina in allowing the conflict to develop, and expressed the fear that the fighting could degenerate into a third world war. Even the *Washington Post*, which immediately took the conflict seriously, referred to it on 5 May as 'this still hard-to-believe war'.

Of course, when the beachhead had been established and the fighting started on the islands such speculation became somewhat academic.

Towards the end of the war it was even eclipsed by the Israeli assault on the Lebanon. Moreover, the unexpectedly swift conclusion of the war put an end to much of the comment. It might have been hard to believe to begin with, but world opinion quickly adjusted and then moved on.

SEVEN

Epilogue

In Britain news of victory in the South Atlantic was greeted with great enthusiasm, and the Prime Minister, after speaking to the media, went off to speak to the joyous crowd waiting outside Downing Street and singing 'Rule Britannia'. When the big ships returned in mid-July they were greeted by flag-waving crowds. On 26 July a ceremony was held in Westminster Abbey to commemorate those who had given their lives during the campaign. A victory parade was organised in London on 12 October 1982, at which Thatcher took the salute of the returning heroes. On various occasions she made speeches about the new mood she perceived in Britain, a mood of new-found confidence, a Falklands factor that had put the 'great' back into Great Britain.

There was criticism, too. The House of Commons Defence Committee announced an enquiry into the handling of the media even before the conflict had ended. Shortly after the end of the conflict, Thatcher also announced the details of the enquiry she had promised into the Government's handling of affairs leading up to the Argentine invasion. The committee was chaired by Lord Franks, a former senior civil servant, diplomat and distinguished academic with considerable experience in chairing committees of enquiry. It presented its report in January 1983, and concluded that it 'would not be justified in attaching any criticism or blame to the present Government for the Argentine junta's decision to commit its act of unprovoked aggression in the invasion of the Falkland Islands on 2 April 1982.' It was quickly pointed out that the body of the report seemed to suggest a somewhat different conclusion. While the British Government could clearly not be blamed for the Argentine junta's decision to invade the islands – taken in circumstances of some precipitation anyway – it could be accused, to borrow an expression used by Callaghan, of having taken its eye off the ball, resulting in 'an unnecessary war'. It had sent mis-leading signals to the junta, and had failed to take sufficiently vigorous action to prevent Argentine frustration at the slow progress on the diplomatic front from boiling over into military action.

In 1982 much of the blame was placed on the Foreign and Commonwealth Office, but the Franks

Report shows that this was a rather hasty judgement. The truth of the matter was that the Falkland Islands dispute was never considered sufficiently critical to discuss it in Cabinet once the Ridley leaseback initiative had been rejected. With hindsight it seems abundantly clear that Britain either had to take unpopular measures to seek a transfer of sovereignty to Argentina of some kind, or, failing that, to provide the resources to defend the islands and to demonstrate that Britain would not hesitate to take appropriate military action if necessary.

At the general election of 1983 Thatcher's Conservative Party won a landslide victory. It was generally believed that the Falklands factor had played a major role, although the divisions within the Opposition, which split the anti-Conservative vote, were also a significant feature. It has been argued that the slight economic upturn that had begun to make itself felt in early 1982 would have led to a Conservative victory anyway. There can be little doubt, however, that there *was* a Falklands factor, which, if nothing else, contributed hugely to Thatcher's personal political standing.

Controversy developed over the circumstances in which the *General Belgrano* was sunk. The Labour MP Tam Dalyell asked an unprecedented number of parliamentary questions on this subject. Leaked information suggested that the cruiser was not 'closing on elements of the task force', as John Nott had announced in the House of Commons, but had in fact been sailing away from the Falklands. The Government went to great lengths to maintain that the cruiser was sailing towards the task force, for reasons which are still not entirely clear. A 'conspiracy theory' gradually emerged according to which the British Government had authorised the attack on the ageing cruiser to scuttle the peace negotiations being put together by the Peruvian President. The new Defence Minister, Michael Heseltine, ordered a secret report to be prepared on what had happened. The civil servant who was given this job was distressed by what he saw as a deliberate attempt to mislead Parliament and he decided to leak the contents to Tam Dalyell. He was charged with breaking the Official Secrets Act, but was acquitted. A report was published in 1985 by the House of Commons Defence Committee on the events of the weekend of 1–2 May 1982.

It seems, although some would still contest this, that the cruiser and its Exocet-carrying escort did represent at least a potential threat, although at the time the *Belgrano* was sunk it was indeed sailing westwards towards a waiting circle off the extreme southern tip of South America. Thatcher and other members of the War Cabinet have argued convincingly that they were extremely sensitive to any risk to the men of the task force and have asked how public opinion would have responded if they had refused to allow the attack and if the task force had then suffered heavy casualties as a consequence. It is also clear that the decision to alter the Rules of Engagement was taken on the basis of information that the cruiser was sailing towards the task force; the Prime Minister was apparently not informed of the change of course. Admiral Lewin has argued that the *course* was only of limited relevance; what mattered was the *position* of the cruiser.

Besides, there is no convincing or conclusive evidence that London had been informed about progress on the Peruvian peace plan when the attack was authorised, and in any case the Peruvian peace plan offered nothing substantially different to the terms rejected only a few days earlier by the junta.

In the Falklands Rex Hunt was returned, although to begin with not as Governor, but as Civil Commissioner, alongside a military commissioner with responsibility for the substantial garrison on the islands. A national holiday was created, 14 June, Liberation Day. Thatcher visited the islands in 1983 and was given a warm welcome. In 1985 a new constitution was introduced, increasing the number of democratically elected representatives on the Executive and Legislative Councils. Rex Hunt (now Sir Rex) then became Governor of the Falkland Islands once again.

A Falkland Islands Development Corporation was set up with a substantial budget, although perhaps this was less than some people had hoped. A major airfield was built, as well as roads to service it and link Stanley with Goose Green, and new hospital facilities provided. Revenue from fishing licences has been substantial in recent years, and a number of licences have been granted to oil companies. Exploratory drilling in the 1990s found some potentially oil-bearing geological formations, and some traces of hydrocarbons were discovered, but low prices in the 1990s meant that oil from the South Atlantic was unlikely to be economically viable in the foreseeable future, and it remains to be seen whether the oil reserves really are as important as has been suggested. There has also been some limited development of tourism on the islands. The decline in the population has been arrested, even excluding the effects of the military population. In short, the bleak economic outlook before the war has changed markedly for the better.

In Argentina reaction against the ruling junta was swift. Galtieri was replaced as President by General

Bignone, with a brief to prepare the country for a return to democracy. In October 1983 the Radical Raúl Alfonsín was elected President and introduced sweeping economic reforms. He said Argentina would seek a peaceful solution to the issue of sovereignty of the Falkland Islands, but re-asserted Argentina's claims. Talks between Britain and Argentina organised in Berne in 1984 foundered almost immediately as a result of a disagreement as to whether sovereignty should be discussed.

In the United Nations support for Argentina over the question of sovereignty returned, with, for example, the United States voting a resolution that called for the two parties to negotiate, bearing in mind the islanders' interests. Thatcher had no intention of negotiating any sovereignty into Argentine hands. She was personally very much opposed to it, and it would no doubt have been politically unacceptable anyway. The islanders themselves could hardly be expected to have become more sympathetic towards Argentina after being invaded, although the gradual progress of Argentina towards democracy was encouraging. International sympathy for Britain's position gradually weakened as the years went by.

In 1989 Alfonsín's economic policies had all but collapsed (inflation reached a colossal 4,000 per cent), and the presidential elections were won by the Peronist Carlos Menem. Menem oversaw a gradual thaw in Anglo-Argentine relations, although while he explicitly rejected the use of force he always made it clear that Argentina would never abandon its sovereignty claims. Diplomatic relations were re-established in 1990.

During Menem's second term, from 1995 to 1999, relations between Argentina and Britain over the Falkland Islands continued to improve. Britain and Argentina signed an agreement in 1995 over joint oil exploration and exploitation around the Falklands. In 1998 talks were held and visits arranged from both sides. Menem visited London, and Prince Charles visited Buenos Aires and the Falklands. In 1999 the first Argentine tourists were allowed into the Falklands, despite protests from the staunchly anti-Argentine section of the Falkland population. In October 1999 the first direct flight from Argentina since the war in 1982 landed at Mount Pleasant airport. Also in October 1999 Thatcher confirmed how important Chilean support for Britain had been in 1982, above all radar information that had given some warning of Argentine air attacks. Indeed it has been argued that it was during the temporary interruption of that service for essential and overdue maintenance that the attack on the landing ships at

111

Fitzroy took place. The suggestion is that Chilean radar information could have helped prevent this major blow to the British forces.

The presidential elections of 24 October 1999 saw a landslide victory for Fernando de la Rua, leading an opposition alliance, and he pledged to reduce unemployment and corruption. The Falkland Islands were not a prominent election issue. Menem's Foreign Minister, Guido di Tella, said that he would like to visit the Falklands. He had conducted a 'charm offensive' on the Falklanders, sending them Christmas presents of books and tapes.

There is little prospect of an early transfer of sovereignty to Argentina. The Labour government under Tony Blair has made it quite clear that any such transfer could not be considered without the approval of the islanders, and that still seems an impossibly unlikely prospect in the near future. Argentina remains convinced that the islands are rightfully theirs. It can still be hoped that Anglo-Argentine relationships, and even links between the islanders and the Argentines, will continue to improve, although progress will inevitably take time, but, fundamentally, the underlying conflict remains.

Further Reading

There have been so many books on the Falklands War that it is particularly difficult to suggest a selection. One of the best of the first wave of books published almost immediately after the conflict is Paul Eddy et al., *The Falklands War: The Full Story by the Sunday Times Insight Team* (London, 1982). However, arguably the best, and most readily available, book on the Falklands War remains Max Hastings and Simon Jenkins, *The Battle for the Falklands* (London, 1983). Also of interest is Martin Middlebrook, *Operation Corporate* (London, 1982), republished in 1987 as *Task Force: The Falklands War, 1982*. The same author studied the war from the Argentine viewpoint in *The Fight for the 'Malvinas'* (London, 1989). Lawrence Freedman and Virginia Gamba Stonehouse, *Signals of War: The Falklands Conflict of 1982* (London, 1990) looks closely at the conflict from both sides, and shows not only the deep conflict of interests but also the many misunderstandings, misperceptions and miscalculations that affected diplomats and politicians both before and during the war, as well as the highly unpredictable nature of war itself. Lawrence Freedman is also the author of a shorter history entitled *Britain and the Falklands War* (London, 1988). There have been a number of television programmes, some of which are still available as cassettes, such as the BBC's *Task Force South* (London, 1982). ITV's *The Untold Story* included interviews that have been published in Michael Bilton and Peter Kosminsky, *Speaking Out: Untold Stories from the Falklands War* (London, 1989).

Further Reading

Channel Four's programme *The Falklands War* was accompanied by a book of the same name by Denys Blakeway (London, 1991). An academic conference was organised on the Falklands War at Keele in 1990: a collection of papers is published in Alex Danchev, *International Perspectives on the Falklands Conflict* (London, 1992), including a stimulating discussion by Lawrence Freedman of the way the theory of escalation led to a misunderstanding of the events of the naval battle at the beginning of May. The role of the SAS is recounted in Ken Connor, *Ghost Force* (London, 1998). Ruben O. Moro, *The History of the South Atlantic Conflict* (New York, 1989) gives an Argentine account of the events in the Malvinas.

The British specialist on the early history of the Falklands and the sovereignty dispute is Peter Beck, author of *The Falkland Islands as an International Problem* (London, 1988). The classic study of sovereignty over the Falklands, first published in 1927 and re-issued in 1982, is Julius Goebels, *The Struggle for the Falkland Islands* (Yale, 1982).

An extremely valuable specialist history focusing on the Navy's contribution is David Brown, *The Royal Navy and the Falklands War* (London, 1987). Similarly, for the air war, Rodney Burdon et al., *Falklands – The Air War* (London, 1986). Readers interested particularly in the land battles will find detailed accounts in Nicholas van der Bijl, *Nine Battles to Stanley* (London, 1999). A comprehensive account of the battle of Goose Green is given in Mark Adkin, *Goose Green* (London, 1992). The political dimension is well portrayed in G.M. Dillon, *The Falklands, Politics and War* (London, 1989). An account of the Argentine political dimension can be found in Oscar Cardoso et al., *The Secret Plot* (English translation, London, 1983).

A large number of servicemen who took part in the campaign have written about their experience of the war. Among these, one might recommend Admiral Sandy Woodward, *One Hundred Days* (London, 1992), Julian Thompson, *No Picnic* (London, 1985), Nick Vaux, *March to the South Atlantic* (London, 1986), Commander 'Sharkey' Ward, *Sea Harrier over the Falklands* (London, 1993), Ewen Southby Tailyour, *Reasons in Writing* (London, 1993), Nick Barker, *Beyond Endurance* (London, 1997) and John and Robert Lawrence, *When the Fighting is Over: a Personal Story of the Battle for Tumbledown Mountain and its Aftermath* (London, 1988). Vincent Bramley, *Excursion to Hell* (London, 1991) tells the story of the battle for Mount Longdon, and includes highly controversial allegations about possible war crimes. An idea of the way the war was seen by Argentine conscripts is given in Daniel Kon, *Los Chicos de la Guerra* (English translation, Sevenoaks, 1983).

Politicians and diplomats have also contributed their accounts. Again, selection is difficult, but of particular interest are Margaret Thatcher, *The Downing Street Years* (London, 1993), Lord Carrington, *Reflect on Things Past* (London, 1988), Nicholas Henderson, *Mandarin* (London, 1994), Rex Hunt, *My Falkland Days* (London, 1992) and Alexander M. Haig, *Caveat* (New York, 1984). An excellent collection of interviews of diplomats and politicians is provided in Michael Charlton, *The Little Platoon: Diplomacy and the Falklands Dispute* (London, 1989).

Media coverage of the conflict has been studied in a number of books, including Robert Harris, *Gotcha!* (London, 1983), Derek Mercer et al., *The Fog of War* (London, 1987), Valerie Adams, *The Media and the Falklands Campaign* (London, 1986), David Morrison and Howard Tumber, *Journalists at War* (London, 1988) and the Glasgow University Media Group, *War and Peace News*

(Milton Keynes, 1985). European opinion is surveyed in Stelios Stavridis and Christopher Hill (eds), *Domestic Sources of Foreign Policy* (London, 1996).

Official reports on the Falklands often make fascinating reading. In particular, the Franks Report, reprinted with an introduction by Alex Danchev as Alex Danchev (ed.), *The Franks Report* (London, 1992), gives a very good account of the development of the crisis from the 1960s until 1982.

Finally, I would like to apologise to all those whose books are not included here, and also take this opportunity to acknowledge the debt I owe to these and other authors whose works have been extremely valuable in the research for this book. I would have preferred to indicate sources in footnotes, but the format of this series precludes such academic references. My sincere thanks to all.

Acknowledgements

My thanks to all those whose work and time has been invaluable in the preparation of this book. Some of them are mentioned in the suggested reading. Others remain anonymous. I am immensely grateful to all. My particular gratitude goes to Asa Briggs, for his enthusiasm and energy. I dedicate this book to Odile, Alice, David, Mum and Dad.

Index

INDEX